BLACKPOOL
AND
THE FYLDE

BLACKPOOL
FOR HEALTHY, HAPPY HOLIDAYS
TRAVEL IN COMFORT BY LMS

SEND FOR FREE GUIDE TO W. T. FOSTER, TOWN HALL, BLACKPOOL.

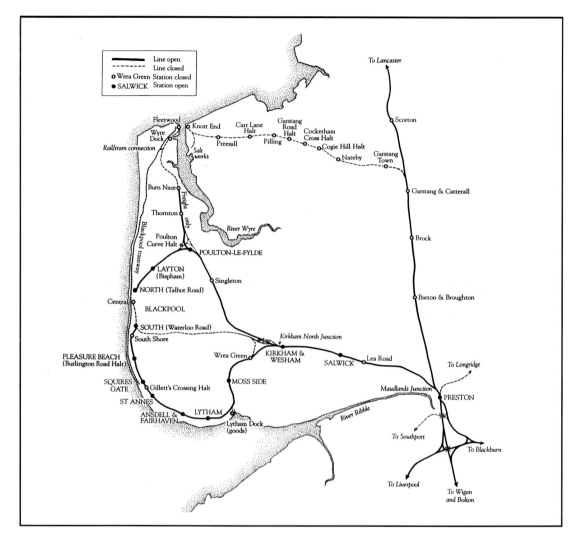

Map of the railways of the Fylde, showing the triple-pronged approach to Blackpool from Kirkham, which irreversibly shaped the coast's geography. The coastal line meanders to the south, the Marton Line heads directly to the heart of the town and the northern route does a virtual 90-degree turn at Poulton, whence the line to Fleetwood heads due north. Across the River Wyre, the Garstang & Knott End railway links the small settlements of this largely agricultural belt of land. Today the Marton and Knott End lines are gone, leaving just the two passenger approaches to Blackpool and the former Fleetwood line as a freight-only spur from Poulton to Burn Naze. There have been more than 40 stations in the Fylde in the past 150 years – today there are 12.

A nostalgic look at the

RAILWAYS
OF
BLACKPOOL
AND
THE FYLDE

Britain's premier resort

Barry McLoughlin

• RAILWAY HERITAGE •
from
The NOSTALGIA Collection

To Joanne, Lisa, Jennie and Barry

First published in July 1996
New edition first published May 1999

British Library Cataloguing in Publication Data

A catalogue record for this book is available from the British Library.

ISBN 1 85794 124 1

Silver Link Publishing Ltd
The Trundle
Ringstead Road
Great Addington
Kettering
Northants NN14 4BW

Tel/Fax: 01536 330588
email: sales@slinkp-p.demon.co.uk

Printed and bound in Great Britain

A Silver Link book
from
The NOSTALGIA *Collection*

ACKNOWLEDGEMENTS

The author wishes to thank the many people who have helped in the preparation of this book, and especially: Paul and Carol Nettleton, Malcolm Richardson, Vernon Smith and Blackpool & Fylde Rail Users' Association; the library and photographic departments of the *Evening Gazette*, Blackpool; Lancashire Library; Barry Shaw and Blackpool Civic Trust; Anthony Coppin, Jack Fenton, Jim Peden, Don Rutter and Tim Shuttleworth; Will Adams of Silver Link for encouragement and editorial expertise; and, for their forbearance, his family. Where no source is given, pictures are from the author's collection.

Half title On the stations of the vast London, Midland & Scottish Railway network, one name figured almost as prominently as that of the company itself: Blackpool and its satellites were emblazoned across most of the stations on Britain's biggest railway company. The Lancashire & Yorkshire Railway, which had always been heavily dependent on the east-west holiday trade, had been active in promoting Blackpool's benefits at its stations, but after 1923 LMS senior managers, aware of the power of large-scale advertising, trumpeted the virtues of the Fylde Coast even more vociferously. Ashton Davies, Chief Commercial Manager of the LMS, proclaimed: 'This vast organisation has done much ... to foster the development of the Fylde and its coastal resorts. There are few of its 2,500 passenger stations throughout the country which do not display in some prominent position a pictorial appeal to the public to visit Blackpool, Cleveleys, Lytham, St Annes, or other places in the Fylde.'

Posters became an increasingly important weapon in the battle for business. At first unsophisticated and cluttered, they were developed by artists like Norman Wilkinson into an art form of their own. But the artists tried to avoid publicity about their involvement, as they regarded them as hack work used mainly to earn money between commissions. In 1994 this LMS poster *circa* 1935 by Claude Buckle, featuring Blackpool's North Shore, was auctioned at Christie's for several hundred pounds. *Christie's*

CONTENTS

RAILWAYS OF BLACKPOOL AND THE FYLDE

1.
RAILS TO BLACKPOOL

Golden Mile gateway

If Blackpool Tower were laid on its side to the south, its tip would touch the former entrance to a long-vanished institution on which the success of the resort's legendary landmark was founded. For 70 years – from 1894 to 1964 – Blackpool Central Station was effectively the entrance to the 518 ft 9 in Tower for millions of holidaymakers. By a poignant piece of timing, however, the 1994 centenary year of Blackpool Tower marked another, less memorable milestone. The resort's Festival '94 coincided with the 30th anniversary of the closure of Central – the terminus that, more than anything else, created the Tower as a tourist attraction. The station, a pivotal piece of Blackpool's heritage and its transport infrastructure, was the main railway gateway to the Golden Mile, siphoning tens of millions of tourists directly on to Britain's most celebrated stretch of promenade.

More than a century of railway and holiday history lies buried beneath the town's central car park in the shadow of the Tower; the solidly paved platform edges of Central are still visible beneath the wheels of the ranks of parked cars, mute memorials to the resort's railway heyday. Only the glazed-roof toilet block and a few foreshortened walls bear witness to what was once one of Britain's busiest railway termini.

Left All lines lead to the Tower: the approaches to Blackpool Central before its closure in 1964, showing the swathe of sidings between Bloomfield and Waterloo Roads. *Evening Gazette*

Two years after the Festival, however, 1996 saw a more upbeat anniversary: Blackpool's Rail 150. Trains had first arrived in the resort on 29 April 1846, with the opening of a 3½-mile branch from the Preston & Wyre Railway at Poulton; the P&W had opened to Fleetwood in 1840. A deal with local landowner Thomas Clifton allowed the branch to run along a corridor of his estate roughly parallel to Talbot Road. The branch's opening was celebrated with a flag-bedecked special train, which carried local dignitaries along the line 24 hours before it entered service to the public. It ran to a handsome but spartan terminus, with a Roman Ionic-style stone portico, on the brow of a gentle hill opposite the Talbot Hotel. By 1866 the line had been converted to double track and the following year a station was opened at Bispham (now Layton).

The Blackpool branch completed a pincer movement that had begun with the opening on 16 February 1846 of a 4¾-mile link from Kirkham to Lytham. The terminus at the latter place was similar to the Blackpool station, with an impressive octagonal booking hall. Intermediate stations were sited at Wray Green (as Wrea Green was spelled until 1875) and Moss Side, and a spur served Lytham Dock. It was 17 years later, on 6 April 1863, that Central came on to the scene as little more than a cabin called Hounds Hill Station, the northern terminus of the Blackpool & Lytham Railway. The 7½-mile single track linked Hounds Hill with a stone-built terminal station in Lytham via an intermediate halt at South Shore. Victorian historian John Porter described the carnival-style celebrations surrounding the official opening of the line, two days before it entered public service:

'The railway was virtually finished in the autumn of 1862, but the formal opening was postponed until the 4th of April, 1863. At that date, which occurred on Saturday, flags and banners floated from many of the windows, whilst the bells of St Cuthbert's Church rang out merry peals at intervals throughout the day. No further ceremony was observed on the occasion, than the running of a train to Blackpool and back with a select party of invited guests.'

For 101 years the station stood on the 23-acre site, wedged between the seafront and Central Drive, almost single-handedly transforming the town from a coastal backwater into Europe's top tourism resort. Hordes of holidaymakers funnelled through its barriers, emerging to the smell of salt spray and candyfloss. But on the misty evening of 1 November 1964, the final day of the Illuminations, the last train pulled out of Central and – claim many critics – signalled the beginning of a downhill gradient for the Fylde's railway services, and possibly even the town itself.

The closure of Central Station – against the recommendation of the Beeching Report – rocked railway supporters and gouged the heart from the resort. More than 30 years on it still provokes resentment. But the shell-shocked reaction could hardly have been predicted from the line's humble origins in 1863. At first it had no physical connection with the P&W at either Blackpool or Lytham. But in 1871 the P&W was sold to the Lancashire & Yorkshire (L&Y) and London & North Western (LNWR) railways as joint proprietors, and on 1 July 1874 the new owners opened a double-track connecting line to the branch from Kirkham at Lytham, bypassing the town's original terminus, which became a goods station.

Presciently, Porter predicted that the coast

A rare picture of a tranquil Central Station soon after its rebuilding at the turn of the 20th century, with the Tower, only a few years old, dominating the background. *Evening Gazette*

line from Kirkham through Lytham St Annes to Blackpool would eventually supersede the old route from Poulton. With the opening of the new Blackpool Central Station at Easter 1901, the coastal line did indeed supplant the route to Blackpool North as the premier line for express trains to London and other major population centres.

Hounds Hill had been renamed Blackpool Central in June 1878, when it comprised four timber platforms and a turntable, while the original resort station had been restyled Blackpool (Talbot Road) in 1872. In 1883 Central's wooden platforms were replaced by stone flags supported on brick walls. By the turn of the century, however, it was clear that a more capacious station would be needed, and a rebuilding scheme began in 1899. The work was completed two years later, providing almost 9,000 feet of regular and excursion platforms, a new station building, engine shed and eventual widening of the approach roads from South Shore.

A railwaymen's hostel was built in Central Drive providing separate rooms for 45 men. It was characteristically solid outside and ascetic inside, although the accommodation was in separate cubicles and there was a plentiful supply of bathwater and a reading room. Even the hostel became overloaded and sometimes sleeping carriages had to be provided for the overspill staff.

Evidence of the scale of the passenger traffic handled by Blackpool's two termini was provided by the doyen of Fylde railwayman, Ashton Davies, in a paper to the meeting of the British Association for the Advancement of Science in Blackpool in 1936. Davies, who was awarded the OBE for his services to the railway, pioneered Blackpool's excursion traffic between the wars. A former stalwart of the Lancashire & Yorkshire, he became Chief Commercial Manager of the London, Midland & Scottish Railway (LMS) after the Grouping in 1923 and later Vice-President of the company. (The effect of the Railways Act of 1921 was to bring all the Fylde's lines – run by the L&Y, LNWR and the tiny Garstang & Knott End – under a single management.) Although he eventually transferred to London

Euston, he remained faithful to Lancashire and never moved his home from Lytham St Annes.

In his article – part of a collection of papers under the title 'A Scientific Survey of Blackpool and District' – he said that the number of passengers reaching Blackpool and adjacent resorts by rail reached the huge total of almost six million a year, excluding the thousands of journeys by season ticket holders who lived in the area.

'During the week preceding August Bank Holiday 1935, the number of passengers passing through the station barriers exceeded half a million, while during the period of the Illuminations – that is, after the normal summer season had ended – the visitors arriving by rail were in the vicinity of 750,000,' he wrote.

Kirkham North Junction could aptly be termed the hub of the Fylde, said Davies, as the signal box there dealt with almost 600 trains in a 24-hour period, averaging one every 2½ minutes. 'The frequency was, of course, much higher during the peak periods, as in the early hours of the day traffic is comparatively light.'

A generation later, in the space of less than 4 hours on 1 August 1964, at the peak of the Glasgow Fair holiday, railway writer and photographer Chris Gammell recorded no fewer than six Blackpool-Scotland trains passing over Shap Summit in Cumbria. Fittingly, a frequent sight toiling up the incline – high point of the West Coast Main Line – was 'Patriot' Class 4-6-0 No 45524 Blackpool, often double-heading with another engine.

But the real pressure began when the Blackpool-bound trains reached their destination and had to be unloaded, turned round and stabled ready for the return journey in the evening. Within a mile of Central Station there was siding space for no fewer than 40 complete trains in the Spen Dyke, Bloomfield Road and Waterloo Road yards – a total of 22 miles of track. Blackpool North could boast storage space for a further 16 full trains. When these were both full, stock was stabled at St Annes, Ansdell and Fairhaven, Lytham, Kirkham, Preston, Lostock Hall and even Horwich near Bolton.

Today Blackpool's railway stations are virtually deserted between midnight and dawn,

THE WEATHER OUTLOOK
Sunny periods
LIGHTS: 10-4, 4-32

WEST LANCASHIRE EVENING GAZETTE

LAST

No. 10906.   WEDNESDAY, JULY 15, 1964.   Tel. 25231   PRICE 4d.
(After 6-30 p.m. 25231)

Station to close after Lights

END OF LINE FOR CENTRAL IS NOW OFFICIAL

A Tower-top view of the Central Station area.

Lancashire get early setbacks

SOUTHPORT, Wednesday.

LANCASHIRE gave D. R. Worsley, the Oxford University captain, his first championship game of the season against Surrey at Southport, and the young left-hander partnered Green when Grieves won the toss and batted first.

Heavy overnight rain delayed the start for half an hour, but the pitch had been protected and

Scoreboard

LANCASHIRE (1st inn)

D. GREEN c Arnold	1
D. WORSLEY not out	28
G. PULLAR b Arnold	20
K. GRIEVES not out	22
Extras	6
Total (2 wkts)	**80**

played easily enough when Gibson and Arnold shared the new ball.

Green took a single from Gibsons first over, but Arnold's third delivery beat and bowled him middle stump as he pushed forward half-heartedly.

Pullar began with two singles into the covers, and the wet outfield plainly robbed the strokes of their full value.

Pullar hit the first boundary with an edged shot wide of slip against the hostile Arnold, but the early dismissal of Green forced Lancashire to go slowly, and they were still struggling in the "twenties" at the end of the first hour.

Worsley played and missed several times before getting off the mark with a single and his two down to fine-leg from Gibson.

Fortunately for Lancashire, Pullar appeared to be in good form and when Surrey switched from Arnold to Storey at 21 Pullar glanced the new bowler well.

Harman came on for a couple of overs, but Worsley off-drove his first delivery to the boundary, and the young spinner was quickly replaced by Arnold.

Worsley took a second boundary with a well-placed on-drive from Storey, but at 48 Surrey secured their second wicket when Arnold forced Pullar to play on.

Minister gives his approval

MR. KENYATTA

Kenyatta unhurt in attempted attack

LONDON, Wednesday.

MR JOMO KENYATTA, the 74 - year - old Prime Minister of Kenya, escaped unhurt today after a man tried to attack him as he was leaving his London hotel.

Mr Kenyatta was about to step into his car, accompanied by a Special Branch man and his own aides, when a man rushed down the pavement "like an express train," said a spokesman of the Hilton Hotel, Park-lane.

He crashed into the group, which cannoned into Mr Kenyatta's car, damaging its side.

A uniformed policeman baulked the attempt by deflecting the man's rush.

He knocked him aside, and police security men closed in.

Two men are expected to appear in court later today.

BLACKPOOL CENTRAL STATION IS TO CLOSE. That is now official as the Minister of Transport (Mr Ernest Marples) has approved British Railways' closure proposals.

But it will not close before the end of the Illuminations. The actual closing date will be announced later, say British Railways today.

Mr Marples has ruled that the closure should not take place unless and until certain bus services on routes 4 and 5 have been revised.

The revisions apply to week-day services to link with the unadvertised workmen's train services from Blackpool South Station (at present leaving Blackpool Central at 5-19 p.m) to serve Mereside, Pilling-crescent and Halfway House.

To sell, to let or to develop . . .

Estate and Service No 5 from Pilling - crescent and Halfway House.

Links will also be required with the return service to Blackpool South (at present arriving at Blackpool Central at 5-19 p.m) to serve Mereside, Pilling-crescent and Halfway House.

Other conditions

Mr Marples puts other conditions on the closure.

They are that the British Railways shall notify the Minister of any proposals for withdrawing or reducing any of the 4, 5, 6, 6a, 12, 13, 22, 22a, 23, 23a, 25 and 25a Blackpool Corporation services, the 11, 11a and 11c operated jointly with Lytham St Annes

To Page 17

ASKED about the future of the railways-owned land between Hounds Hill and Waterloo-road, including the Central Station site, a British Railways spokesman in Manchester said today that when it had been decided what land would not be needed for railway purposes, the railways' estates department

would either offer it for sale or to let to the best commercial advantage or develop it themselves.

He said that it was not possible at this stage to state how much of the land in the mile and a quarter between the two stations would be needed for railway purposes when South Station became the terminus.

40 acres

THE area of land owned by British Railways between Hounds Hill and Waterloo-road, including Central Station, was about 40 acres, said a Blackpool Surveyor's Department spokesman this afternoon.

Chancellor intervenes in postal dispute

LONDON, Wednesday.

MR REGINALD MAUDLING, the Chancellor of the Exchequer, intervened today in the postmen's dispute — but he was not expected to make a new pay offer.

The Treasury said this afternoon: "The Chancellor

To Back Page

What they say today

HERE are today's views on the Central Station announcement:

Mr Harry Porter
Blackpool Director of Attractions and Publicity

This decision will now crystallise the whole position of the development of this important area of Blackpool.

I think it will ultimately prove to the advantage of Blackpool.

We are certainly not going to be lacking in facilities for rail passengers.

Coun L. Greenwood
President of Blackpool Chamber of Trade

I think the closure will be a good thing, and the sooner the better. Then we can get on with some redevelopment to the centre of the town.

The longer we wait the more it will take to get things cleared up. Traffic is increasing day by day without anything being done

ways, but the volume of traffic they bring also brings its problems. The town is now congested all the time.

But now we can get on with clearing the problem, and the railways have plenty of scope for development at South Shore Station

Mrs Pearl Leishman
President of Blackpool Hotel and Boardinghouse Association

I welcome it, providing that South Station is improved to deal with the extra numbers of passengers, and that bus services are improved.

I don't think that boarding-houses will suffer.

Mrs E. M. Ham
Chairman of the Blackpool Private Hotels Association

I think the station's closing will prove to be very beneficial to Blackpool in the long run.

We can get all the visitors we

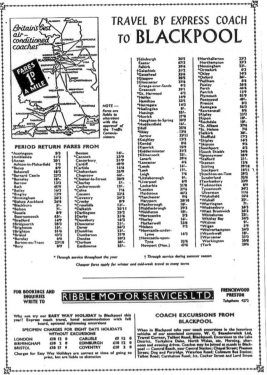

Above Road versus rail – adverts from a 1958 Blackpool holiday guide.

Left Central sensation: the *Evening Gazette* front page of 15 July 1964 announcing Transport Minister Ernest Marples's approval of the station's closure. The newspaper reported that it was almost universally welcomed by the town's tourism and business interests.

but during the era of railway supremacy activity went on through the night. No fewer than 14 trains departed after midnight on 20 September 1952, the last at 1.55 am. These were the days when travellers thought nothing of rising at 4 am to catch an early-morning excursion and return in the small hours, to maximise their time in the resort.

The return fare on the 'Dance Special' was half a crown (2s 6d, or 12½p) and an extra threepence gained admission to the Tower or the Winter Gardens' Empress Ballroom.

Barrow boys transported the luggage of passengers who could not, or would not, pay for a taxi. Cries of 'Carry your cases, Madam?' echoed around Central and North Stations as trains arrived and luggage-laden holidaymakers

disembarked. The carts were usually home-made, improvised from spare parts of prams and trolleys. The going rate was a tanner (sixpence) or a bob (1 shilling).

But by the 1950s the rise of the internal combustion engine was already taking its toll, even on the Fylde's flourishing railway system. Well before the beginning of mass car ownership, the motor bus had been a significant competitor to the railway. The main express bus route, the X60, which ran from Manchester to Blackpool, was in its heyday the busiest of its kind in the world. In the 1950s the timetable had a bus leaving Manchester for Blackpool every 15 minutes on summer Saturdays, and a continuous stream of coaches headed to the coast from central and east Lancashire. The competition was thrown into sharp perspective by the fact that the main bus station was just across Talbot Road from Blackpool North.

When Dr Richard Beeching's report proposed the closure of one of Blackpool's termini in 1963, it was North rather than Central that he chose. Early in 1964, however,

BR stunned the railway community by announcing that Central would shut, with South Station becoming the terminus for London trains. A redevelopment deal had been struck with the Town Council, which for decades had wanted to get rid of the railway from the prime town centre site, and the land was sold for less than £1 million. It was, said some sceptics, the sale of the century.

On the cold, damp night of 1 November, the final train from Central slipped out of platform 3 at 9.55 pm, heading for London Euston. Even on that last day there had been no fewer than 55 departures from the station. The sad spectacle was witnessed by a large crowd of enthusiasts, to the accompaniment of three detonators that had been placed on the track as an unofficial commemoration of the historic event. More than 1½ hours later, the last train to arrive – a diesel from Manchester Victoria – approached the fog-shrouded platforms. Blackpool driver Tom Eastham sounded the hooter before being greeted with a kiss from his wife and a bottle of beer from his son. Then the station gates were locked for the final time. The following day, reported the *Evening Gazette*, the once-bustling station resembled a ghost town.

Within hours of its closure, the systematic demolition of Central Station began, with Post Office engineers moving in first to remove the telephones and bookstall staff sorting through

the stock to be transferred to Blackpool North. Central's main building become a bingo hall and was eventually flattened to make way for the Coral Island complex.

Ernest Ward, who worked for Blackpool Council's building department, had the awkward job of dismantling part of the station's roof. With a workmate, he was detailed to remove unsafe glass roofing, covering what had been some of the platforms before the site was cleared permanently. Happily, the work was completed without any mishaps. In fact, the worst thing Mr Ward and his workmate had to endure was the continual blaring of the contemporary hit 'The Last Waltz' from a funfair opposite the site.

But Mr Ward also had fonder memories of the station and the coastal line from Kirkham. He remembered his first footplate journey as a boy – a hot, headlong trip along the line with his fireman brother in the 1940s – with a mixture of affection and fright.

* * *

Like Roman Gaul, Blackpool was divided into three parts – by the railway. The resort was shaped – socially and physically – by the rail tracks, and they in turn were shaped by the development of the resort. The two lines to Blackpool in the Victorian era determined patterns of commercial and residential

Central may have shut, but as Blackpool celebrated its Festival '94 three decades later, there were at least two pictorial memorials for the station. This limited edition souvenir china plate was produced to commemorate both the Tower milestone and the anniversary of the closure of Central. The plate – titled 'Blackpool Tower and Central

Station Remembered' – measures 10½ inches and was made in the Potteries from Staffordshire white china. All 400 are numbered. The souvenir, produced by Ron Harris of Burton-on-Trent with artwork by David Charlesworth, features yet another Blackpool-based 'Jubilee', No 45705 *Seahorse*, steaming out of Central.

A second pictorial tribute is a magnificent painting of the station in 1960 by Derbyshire-based artist David Wright who, like David Charlesworth, is a member of the Guild of Railway Artists. The signed, limited edition print – 'Summer Showers' – shows two locos simmering and shimmering alongside the glistening platform in the light summer rain. It vividly recaptures the atmosphere of Central just four years before its closure, when the artist himself would not even have started school. The original hung in an exhibition in the Tower viewed by the Queen and Prince Philip. Mr Wright presented the first print to David Upton, Deputy Editor of the *Evening Gazette*, for display in the newspaper's offices. The picture was also made into a 1,000-piece jigsaw by Waddington's. *Ron Harris*

development that are still evident today. The prosperity of the two principal stations' hinterlands reflected shifts in the relative importance attached to each terminus by the railway companies.

The original Blackpool branch scythed through the north and east of the fledgling seaside resort, then the Blackpool & Lytham cut another swathe through the south. As Lytham's Lord of the Manor, Colonel Clifton had been a belated but enthusiastic convert to the idea of a line that would open up new sites for seaside villas on his land. In the event, the link was to have largely the opposite effect, bypassing South Fylde and giving further impetus to Blackpool's development. As in the case of the Preston & Wyre Railway to Fleetwood, Blackpool was almost an accidental beneficiary.

The line profoundly changed the geography of southern Blackpool. It bisected the South Shore community, laying down a physical dividing line between the predominantly tourist areas on the narrow strip to the west of the tracks and the residential district to the east. It is a division that Blackpool Council, more than 130 years later, is still trying to bridge.

These two lines, effectively splitting the resort into three, retained their duopoly until 1903, when a new fast link was opened from Kirkham North Junction to Blackpool Central. Known as the New Line or Marton Line, it allowed trains to run non-stop from Kirkham & Wesham to Blackpool, short-circuiting the more meandering routes to the north and south. At one stage it seemed that the line, measuring almost 7 miles, would have to be abandoned because of a deep bog near Weeton. After 3½ years' work, however, the link was opened following a test run by four heavy locomotives over the Marton Moss section. But the steep ascent from Blackpool South Station to the bridges over Watson Road and Hawes Side Lane still made it a hard pull for a long excursion train packed with passengers.

The Marton Line again helped to shape the geography of Blackpool and the development of its south-eastern suburbs, although the fact that much of it was carried on a heavily bridged embankment meant that it was not as disruptive as the coastal line. The New Line is now occupied by a section of the M55 motorway and the Yeadon Way link road to the South Shore and Central coach and car parks.

The railway continued to expand, and so did the hotels and businesses that depended upon it; clusters of small boarding houses sprouted in the streets around Blackpool North. Yet the debate continues about just how profound an effect the railway had on Blackpool's expansion. One school contends that the railway, while important, was merely a facilitator, an enabler, rather than a creator. This theory's proponents point to the fact that the L&Y was often a grudging provider of mediocre services, and continually had to be prodded and pushed into making improvements. Given the state of Blackpool's communications before the railway age, however – it was a settlement of barely 700 people reached by a rutted and sometimes impassable road from Preston – it is barely credible that the resort could have become Europe's top tourist town without the railway.

The first regular stage coach service between Preston and Blackpool had begun in 1816, but one contemporary traveller recounted the not uncommon experience of leaving Deansgate in Manchester at 8 am and arriving in Blackpool at 6.30 pm. Almost half the journey was occupied by the 17-mile final leg from Preston.

The impression made by the new-fangled railway on natives of the Fylde, accustomed to travelling no quicker than the fastest horse, is vividly recounted in the seminal book *History of the Fylde of Lancashire*. This work by John Porter, published in 1876, gives an exhaustive account of the development of the area up to the reign of Queen Victoria. Porter quotes a verse written by a gentleman resident of the Fylde, Henry Anderton, on the opening of the P&W in 1840, under the pen-name '1st Class':

Some fifty years since and a coach had no
    power,
To move faster forward than six miles an hour,
Till Sawney McAdam made highways as good,
As paving-stones crushed into little bits could…
The Present has taken great strides of the Past,

For carriages run without horses at last!
And what is more strange, – yet it's truth, I
   avow,
Hack-horses themselves have turned passengers
   now!
These coaches alive go in sixes and twelves,
And once set in motion they travel themselves!
They'll run thirty miles while I'm cracking this
   joke,
And need no provisions but pump-milk and
   coke!
And with their long chimneys they skim, o'er
   the rails,
With two thousand hundred-weight tied to
   their tails!
While Jarvey in stupid astonishment stands,
Upturning both eyes and uplifting both hands,
'My nags,' he exclaims, betwixt laughing and
   crying,
'Are good 'uns to go, but yon devils are flying.'

The arrival of the railway telescoped journey times enormously and hugely increased passenger volumes. In the decade from 1863, the number of arrivals at least quadrupled. In 1873 about 850,000 passengers arrived at Blackpool's two rail termini during the season. According to the 1881 Census, however, Blackpool still had fewer than 13,000 residents, making it only the 20th biggest holiday resort. By 1883 the number of rail arrivals had increased by almost half a million, and in the early 1890s was approaching two million. By the start of the new century, the total was fast reaching three million, and on the eve of the First World War it was nearing four million. With a total of 29 platforms between them, North and Central were handling up to 80 excursions a day, in addition to regular traffic.

In 1911 Blackpool had leapfrogged Southport to become the fifth largest resort, with more than 58,000 inhabitants. That amounts to a more than fourfold expansion in 30 years, astonishing by anyone's standards. During the 1930s – when excursion traffic probably reached its peak as war clouds loomed over Europe – the resort's publicity machine was claiming seven million annual visitors – 10,000 times the early 19th-century population of the town.

There is certainly no denying the railway's physical impact on the Blackpool and Fylde landscape. With the lines from Poulton and Lytham approaching Blackpool from opposite ends, it led to an unfocused development of an urban core that appeared to lack a natural centre of gravity. This apparently random and unco-ordinated development was accelerated by shifts in railway company policy. Thirteen years after the opening of the Blackpool & Lytham Railway, the L&Y switched its Manchester express from Talbot Road to Hounds Hill. This move, coupled with an increasing amount of excursion traffic from east Lancashire and the West Riding being routed along the coastal line, dramatically shifted the focal point of Blackpool.

New streets fanned out on the landward side of Central, and in them a fresh crop of purpose-built boarding houses soon blossomed. In the nearby Revoe area, the oldest part of urban Blackpool, working men's clubs sprang up to provide entertainment and recreation both for locals and visitors. They included the LMS Loco Club in Back Ribble Road, which started life as a disused railway carriage.

Meanwhile, as the central district expanded, property values around Talbot Road Station slumped. Worst hit, though, was Blackpool's first major 'inland' holiday attraction, Raikes Hall Gardens, at the eastern end of Church Street. These had initially been so popular that trippers often went straight there from Talbot Road Station and visited no other attraction, while boarding houses in Cookson Street and Topping Street benefited from being on the main pedestrian route to the Raikes. In a desperate bid to entice rail visitors back, Raikes management put up large posters outside Central Station urging tourists to make the half-mile trek to the pleasure gardens. With the Tower just outside the station entrance, however, it was not difficult to predict which of the competing attractions would win the tussle for custom.

The north-south shift of emphasis was further underlined by the rebuilding of Central at the turn of the century. No fewer than 34 parallel sidings served the terminus, occupying a huge belt of land within an ice-cream cone's

The graceful, circular sweep of the Pleasure Beach Casino Building soon after its opening in 1939 to cater for LMS excursionists. This postcard, which also features a trio of open 'boat' trams, is undated, but must be from wartime as on the reverse is printed a stirring quotation from Prime Minister Winston Churchill: 'Let us all strive without failing in faith or in duty'. The helter-skelter (which is purely decorative) obviously symbolises the attractions of an amusement park, but does the circular motif alongside it represent roulette (even though the only gambling was on fruit machines), a ferris wheel – or the railway? *Commercial postcard*

throw of the sea. Even within holiday areas, however, there were subtle changes of emphasis.

When the Blackpool & Lytham opened, there was just one intermediate station, at South Shore. This became the hub of a web of streets; some, like Station Road and Station Terrace, had railway resonances, while others were named after prominent individuals, such as Osborne Road, Withnell Road and Dean Street. However, the opening of the Marton Line 40 years later was accompanied by the construction of a new station, Waterloo Road, only a quarter of a mile to the north. In 1916 Waterloo Road (renamed Blackpool South on 17 March 1932) was converted into a junction station, with an island platform to serve the coast line. South Shore Station, which had become superfluous, was closed on 14 July 1916.

The expanding railway also shifted the Fylde's social focus. The southward drift created resentment in North Shore, which housed the upper-bracket hotels like the Imperial. And the northern part of town failed to regain completely its previous pre-eminence even after the closure of Central in 1964 and the subsequent restoration of InterCity services to Blackpool North.

While the guest houses grouped around the two stations tended to be patronised by working class visitors, the lower-middle and middle classes would gravitate towards more up-market areas like Claremont Park and Queen's Promenade in North Shore. However, the concentration of Manchester and eventually London services at Central led to the decline of areas like Claremont Park. Meanwhile, the opening of salubrious New South Promenade in 1926 meant more business for Waterloo Road station.

Blackpool's boisterous business atmosphere was typified by widespread touting. From the opening of the Poulton to Blackpool branch, landladies or their representatives had accosted visitors at the station, or in the streets outside, to persuade them of the benefits of their establishments. A long but not completely successful campaign against the practice was waged through the second half of the 19th century and into the 20th.

The first tourist touts were probably the proprietors of the small boarding houses that had sprung up in side streets near Talbot Road Station in the mid-19th century. The first impulse of a family emerging from the station entrance and glancing down Talbot Road to the sea was to head straight towards it. Understandably – for their livelihoods were at stake – the boarding house owners tried to persuade them otherwise. As a result, the railway operators enforced a bylaw against interfering with the comfort of passengers in 1869. But this merely drove the touts off the railway property and into the surrounding streets.

As rail services expanded and competition intensified, street traders and itinerant musicians joined the professional persuaders hired by restaurant owners and entertainment companies, making a cacophonous noise around the stations at weekends. The corporation obtained special regulatory powers in 1879, but enforcement remained difficult, and the practice continued well into the 20th century.

* * *

The Fylde Coast was a microcosm of industrial and commercial Britain. While Blackpool was overwhelmingly working class, neighbouring Cleveleys was a resort for those with bourgeois aspirations and Lytham St Annes harboured still grander pretensions. The rural Over Wyre district even contained some genuine gentry, with a lineage dating back to Tudor times. All strata of society either lived, or worked, in the Fylde. And it was the railway that was largely responsible for creating this social pot-pourri.

Nowhere was Blackpool's position as a social melting-pot more apparent than at the Pleasure Beach, another centenarian attraction, founded in 1896 by the pioneering partnership of J. W.

Outhwaite and W. G. Bean. At first it was – literally – a beach, a ramshackle collection of fairground rides, stalls and sideshows on a 42-acre former gipsy encampment on the sands at South Shore. It grew into Europe's biggest amusement park, and is still owned by one family, the Thompsons, descendants of W. G. Bean. In the Pleasure Beach Fun House, until it burned down in 1991, there was a ride called the Social Mixer, which ended up with all the participants in an undistinguished heap in the middle. That was the role, hugely helped by the railway, of the Pleasure Beach and of Blackpool.

The Fun House was designed in the mid-1930s by the renowned modern architect Joseph Emberton, a specialist in reinforced concrete construction. In May 1939 the Pleasure Beach unveiled what was the apex of Emberton's design, the magnificent art deco Casino building. The striking, circular three-storey structure is now regarded as an outstanding example of 1930s architecture, even though the advanced nature of its construction caused some problems during building work, including a partial collapse.

Incredibly, this was the congested scene on platforms 9 and 10 at Central in 1963, barely a year before its closure. Smiling trippers from Oldham flood from a special train in a typical mill-town excursion. *Evening Gazette*

What is less well known is that the Casino – later called the Wonderful World building – was constructed almost solely for rail excursion passengers.

Evidence of this is provided by the fact that the building was opened not by a local worthy or by a Pleasure Beach panjandrum but by Lord Stamp, Chairman of the London, Midland & Scottish Railway Company, who had been granted the freedom of Blackpool two years earlier. Nor did the fact that Blackpool used some of the nation's most acclaimed architects – like Emberton and the theatre designer Frank Matcham – to plan its pleasure palaces strike anyone as curious: nothing was too good for the resort's holidaymakers.

David Cam, Company Secretary and a Director of the Pleasure Beach, explained: 'The building was designed for LMS party bookings. We could seat 1,000 LMS charter passengers down at one time for lunch at noon, 1 pm and 2 pm, for tea at 3 pm, 4 pm and 5 pm, and for dinner any time after that.

'The building was created purely for that, and all the other attractions in the Casino were supplementary.'

The ground and first floors were partitioned into smaller rooms and the partitions could be swung open to create the huge dining areas. The other party bookings were for works outings from the mills, mines and manufacturing plants of Lancashire and Yorkshire. This was in the days when the LMS sought to 'sell' Blackpool at all its stations across the North, with a network of representatives in every community, rather like today's football pools agents. In July 1945, for instance, two weeks before Victory over Japan Day, the LMS carried what it claimed was an all-time record number of passengers into Blackpool, with 102,889 arriving in the resort within 24 hours on the first Wakes Saturday of the season. For millions of millworkers from the east Lancashire and West Riding textile towns, and colliers from the pit villages of south Lancashire and Yorkshire, the noise and sweat of the working day at the looms or mines was made more tolerable by the prospect of boarding a train to spend Wakes Week by the Irish Sea.

An LMS regulation ticket stipulating the date and train on which passengers could travel home from Blackpool.

As long ago as 1870 the resort thought it worthwhile to pay the substantial sum of £1,000 to the L&Y and LNWR to rent advertising hoardings for five years. Giant billboards in the middle of railside fields promised 'High Tides and High Times' during Christmas breaks. The Town Council even telegraphed details of tides and stormy seas to entice still more tourists. Blackpool's enterprising publicity manager, Mr Naden, sent out countrywide telegrams when major events, such as the opening of a pier, were to take place. While today's traveller seeks to 'get away from it all' and meet fresh faces, it was just the opposite in Blackpool. Entire communities were transplanted to the seaside for a week or two.

The unique pattern of Wakes Week holidays in northern England provided a continuous source of business for the fast-expanding resort. Before the arrival of the railway the Wakes were rowdy affairs, with townsfolk making their own raucous fun in their own backyards. These festivities were coupled with religious observances like the rush-bearing services, in which fresh rushes were laid on the earthen floors of local churches. The more secular Wakes were civilised in the mid-Victorian period by the advent of the railway, which allowed workers to decamp to the seaside for a day, a week or even, if they were lucky, a fortnight.

Lancashire had the most densely packed railway system outside London and the highest concentration of manufacturing workers in the country; these two factors proved to be a potent economic combination. In the days before the onset of the package holiday, a week in Blackpool represented a sizeable financial outlay for a mill-town family. Workers saved up

A famous shot of part of the fleet of 17 special trains lining up to take trippers home from Talbot Road after Bass Brewery's mass excursion in 1896, shortly before the terminus was rebuilt. *British Railways*

Edwardian ladies in their crinolines and bonnets stroll along the Esplanade at St Annes in a colour postcard produced by the L&Y in 1907; postcards were as important as posters in spreading the railway message. This view from the pier shows the bandstand, monument and, on the beach, donkeys apparently doing little business.

every week in the holiday clubs run in virtually every northern industrial town. Before Wakes Week, vast amounts of cash were withdrawn from the clubs – cash that would be pumped into the accounts of the railway companies and the developing tourist economies of the Fylde Coast. It all allowed Blackpool to enjoy a uniquely extended summer season as first one inland town, then another, pulled down the shutters and headed for the seaside.

The Wakes holiday excursions to the coast provided a social safety-valve for the toiling masses of the northern mill towns. Marx and Engels could never have predicted that the enlightened self-interest of the employers would find such an ingenious method of maintaining the morale – and the health – of their workforces. Thomas Mawson, the acclaimed architect, who came from Scorton near Garstang and designed Blackpool's Stanley Park, recalled a chat with a well-to-do visitor on the promenade.

'If it wasn't for Blackpool, there'd be a revolution in Lancashire,' the visitor told him. 'Men stick it as long as they can in the mill towns and once a year they must either burst or go to Blackpool. They come back quietened down and ready for work again!'

For a century Blackpool has been the conference capital for trade unions, hosting their annual gatherings and the congress of the TUC. In 1952 the weavers' union in Blackburn celebrated its anniversary by taking all 10,000 members on a day trip to Blackpool.

Employers, starting with the enlightened entrepreneur Richard Cobden in 1846, also staged mass excursions. The biggest was organised in 1896 by brewery company Bass, Gretton and Co of Burton-on-Trent, which ran a procession of special trains to Blackpool, the first leaving at 4.15 am. Another left London at 5 am. In all, 17 trains carried a total of more than 11,000 people to the resort. Bass negotiated a special ticket to the town's attractions in a scheme prefiguring the Pleasure Beach-BR link almost a century later. In 1953 Bury Felt took its entire workforce to Blackpool by train for Coronation celebrations.

In the opposite direction, the railway companies organised excursions to South Shore FC's cup tie at Leicester Fosse in 1894. South Shore lost 2-1 despite dominating much of the game, but a correspondent described the crowd as a 'thoroughly genteel and respectable company'.

There could be any excuse for an excursion. When the town's pioneering Siemens electric lighting system was unveiled on 19 September 1879, dozens of special trains brought tens of thousands of visitors to the town for a grand carnival. Between 75,000 and 100,000 trippers were crammed into the resort, many having to sleep in the open air as Blackpool simply ran out of beds.

Fourteen years later, the resort tried to repeat the panache of the carnival for the opening of the new electricity works by Lord Kelvin, President of the Royal Society and the most eminent electrical engineer of his day. The works was served by sidings branching off the main line at Princess Street. Unfortunately, the incessant rain put a dampener on the celebrations, but thousands of day visitors still made the trip by rail to see the 'Electrical Fete'. The half-day trips organised by the railway companies were particularly well-patronised. It is ironical that a town in which electricity played such a formative role – a symbolic heraldic thunderbolt even features in the resort's coat-of-arms – has never enjoyed the benefits of an electric railway separate from the famous trams.

Three miles down the coast, St Annes, even more than Blackpool, was a creation of the railway. It was a planned residential town developed as a dormitory for businessmen commuting to Blackpool, Preston, east Lancashire and Manchester. Before the arrival of the railway it simply did not exist, and even by 1881 the population was only 1,000. Over the next 30 years, however, it expanded tenfold, and its spacious detached houses became the residences of wealthy Manchester merchants and manufacturers.

In Blackpool, the scale of the weekly rail invasion was colossal. On a single high-season Saturday in 1910, Talbot Road and Central handled 434 arrivals and departures. At Talbot Road alone, 3,000 items of advance luggage were dealt with, requiring several special trains and the use of 40 delivery carts. The problem was just as bad on the return journeys from Blackpool. For some of the most popular services, large crowds would congregate on the platforms at the two termini and there would be an unseemly competition for seats. In an attempt to end the chaos, the L&Y introduced a system of 'regulated' trains. For no extra charge, passengers were issued with supplementary tickets identifying the date and time of the train on which they could travel. Supply was matched to demand and every passenger was assured of a seat. During the 11 weeks that regulation was in force in the 1919 summer season – the first proper holiday break after four years of war – almost a million passengers were carried to Blackpool from Manchester and its satellite towns.

Central Station

A trio of panoramic aerial views, from contemporary postcards, demonstrating how the centre of Blackpool was dominated by its seafront station at the foot of the Tower. In the photograph on the right, taken from the north in about 1950, a plume of smoke identifies an approaching train at Central; in the second (*below*), this time looking from the south, the line of the railway snakes into town from the right, between the two gas-holders. The picture is from the 1920s, and the presence of the giant wheel, to the right of the Tower, indicates that it must have been taken before 1928, when the huge but slow-moving attraction was demolished. The third view (*bottom*), from 1957, clearly shows the swathe of land occupied by the terminus, with its corrugated roof running diagonally south-east of the Tower.

Right The vista that greeted generations of visitors as they poured out of Central Station on to the promenade. The pavement alongside the Golden Mile is packed, although curiously no trams are in view. The concrete anti-invasion blocks on the seafront indicate that the picture must have been taken during or immediately after the Second World War. Central Station lies immediately to the left, with its approach tracks running roughly parallel to the road, and the photograph was taken from the point below which passengers flooded out of Hounds Hill on to the promenade. *Commercial postcard*

Below The extent of competition from the internal combustion engine was already becoming apparent in this between-the-wars shot of Central Drive directly opposite Central Station. Motor coaches left daily for London and Birmingham, as well as on tours to Chester, North Wales, Scotland and the Lakes. In the foreground is the loop in the Central Drive tram route to Waterloo Road. With a sort of perverse symbolism, the multi-storey car park that had risen on the Central Station site following its closure was demolished in autumn 1998 after barely 30 years. In February 1999 plans were announced for a feasibility study into building a major new conference complex on the former station site.

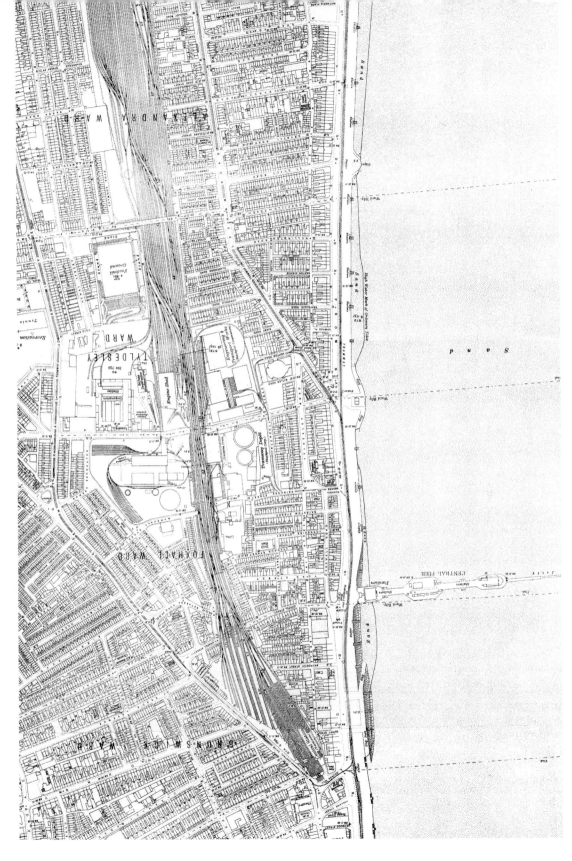

Left This Ordnance Survey map from 1932 again shows the extent to which the southern approaches to Blackpool were dominated by the railway. It has been deliberately inverted to correspond with the photograph opposite; from the bottom can be seen the main station, the excursion platforms, the link to the gasworks, Central shed, the connections to the corporation yard and the tram works, and Spen Dyke, Bloomfield Road and Waterloo Road carriage sidings. *Crown Copyright*

Above This Tower-top view shows the main station with the uncovered excursion platforms on the left. A few hundred yards further south, beyond the platforms, the line borders (right) the municipal electricity and gas works and transport depot and, to the left, the rugby league and football grounds, with Central shed and turntable between them. *Evening Gazette*

RAILWAYS OF BLACKPOOL AND THE FYLDE

An aerial vista showing the vast hinterland of sidings south of Central Station shortly before its closure in 1964, contrasted with a 1973 picture from the opposite direction showing the track lifted and the barren area – now known as the South Shore Central Corridor – ready to be transformed into Europe's biggest coach and car park.
Raymond Hoyle, Evening Gazette

RAILS TO BLACKPOOL

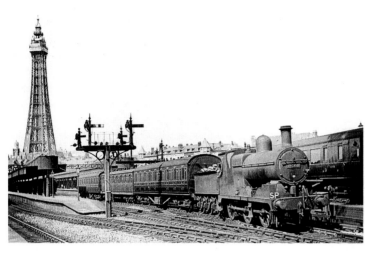

A former L&Y '3F' 0-6-0, LMS No 12560, hauls a three-coach train of varied and elderly stock out of platform 5 at Central Station on a pre-war local service. More modern carriages are in the excursion platforms on the right. The porters' room at the original terminus had been the scene of an historic meeting in the 1880s when John Leach stood up and pleaded with fellow workers to consider setting up a workers' co-operative in the town. After the meeting he canvassed and got 24 names, but most withdrew for fear of dismissal. However, as current Blackpool councillor and Co-operative stalwart Joan Greenhalgh explains, Leach and fellow pioneer Fred Watson held the first meeting of the new Blackpool Co-operative movement at Clarke's Coffee Palace in 1885. *J. A. Peden collection*

A classic view of Manchester-bound ex-LMS 'Black Five' 4-6-0 No 44947 accelerating out of platform 3 at Central a few years before its closure in 1964. *Don Rutter*

RAILWAYS OF BLACKPOOL AND THE FYLDE

By the late 1950s diesel was beginning to replace steam on some Blackpool long-haul services. Here English Electric 2,000 hp Type 4 (later Class 40) diesel-electric No D372 pulls out of platform 2 and prepares to cross Chapel Street bridge bound for London Euston. *Don Rutter*

In gleaming green, a new diesel multiple unit draws out of platform 3 at Central *circa* 1960. The view illustrates some of the most distinctive features of the terminus (from left): the corrugated roof of the main platforms; the water tower at the end of platforms 5 and 6; the stationary heating boilers with their extended chimneys between platforms 6 and 7; and the excursion platforms fronting Central Drive. Local boys – and girls – would congregate outside the station offering to carry holidaymakers' cases, a practice known as 'bagging'. *Don Rutter*

Above An eerily evocative panoramic view of the Central Station platforms immediately after closure; the excursion platforms are on the right. Track, signals and buildings are intact – but there are no trains. The closure operation involved the removal of 39,000 sleepers, 18½ miles of track, 2,310 tons of rails and 1,530 tons of iron chairs. *Evening Gazette*

Below The headline on the seated man's newspaper refers to the rail strike of 1955. That explains why the concourse at Central contains only a handful of passengers, travelling hopefully. Note the hoardings advertising Silver Shred marmalade and Andrews liver salts, amongst others. *Evening Gazette*

It's just before 2.30 on a sunny afternoon in the season, and the crowds bustle around the entrance to Central in this typical postwar scene. A sign beneath the canopy directs trippers to the excursion platforms, 7 to 14, in Central Drive. The seafront is to the right and the famous Burton's Cafe can be seen to the left. *Evening Gazette*

Above Another view of the station entrance in early British Railways days, next to the New Inn and Central Hotel and with Central Pier in the background. Just out of the picture, to the right, is the famous now-demolished Palatine Hotel, with its distinctive third-floor 'turret'. *Evening Gazette*

Below The gasometers and chimneys of the gas and electricity works make this seem more like a scene from an inland industrial town, but it is only yards from Blackpool seafront, with Central Station as its centrepiece. An enclosed Standard tram waits on the short spur of track in Bank Hey Street before turning left to run alongside the station down Central Drive. The picture is undated but must be prewar as the Central Drive route closed in October 1936, when it was replaced by buses. Note the former Feldman's Theatre on the left.

RAILWAYS OF BLACKPOOL AND THE FYLDE

Right LMS 'Jubilee' No 5563 *Australia* leaves Central with a flurry of steam and smoke in a prewar ground-level shot that emphasises the sheer power of the class. A newspaper sub-editor has taken the trouble to delineate the Tower, which had been partly obscured by the fumes and weather! *Evening Gazette*

Right With spectacular exhaust on a frosty winter's morning, and with the sun glinting on its carriages, 'Black Five' 4-6-0 No 45353 announces its arrival at Bloomfield Road on the Central approaches in about 1960. *Don Rutter*

Below 'Royal Scot' Class 4-6-0 *Royal Fusilier*, with the distinctive number 46111, heads out of Central past the water tank at the motive power depot in the early 1960s. *Don Rutter*

Above 'Jubilee' No 45623 *Palestine* trails a plume of steam and smoke as it heads out of Central past the loco shed in the late 1950s. The line was controlled by no fewer than 13 signal boxes – including the apotheosis of them all, the 132-lever giant at Central itself – which were recorded in a definitive study by a local signalling expert, the late Frank Simpson. Today there are just six boxes serving the whole of the Fylde. *Don Rutter*

Left At their peak more than 60 locos were based at Blackpool North and Central sheds. Here, in a scene from early in the 20th century, an unidentified L&Y Aspinall 2-4-2T appears to be the only engine ready for duty at the sprawling Central shed. *J. A. Peden collection*

Left Sir William Stanier's 'Jubilee' Class 4-6-0s of the LMS formed the backbone of Blackpool's express services. A pristine member of the class, No 45653 *Barham*, named after one of the sea lords who helped mastermind the Trafalgar campaign, stands in Rigby Road MPD *circa* 1960. *Don Rutter*

Above The heyday of steam in Blackpool coincided with the glory days of soccer in the town. The train was the main mode of transport for supporters travelling to away matches, and the decline of Central Station presaged a slump in the resort's football fortunes. Blackpool-based 'Jubilee' No 45584 *North West Frontier* stands outside Central shed near the Bloomfield Road football ground. The vast roof covering the Spion Kop (just visible to the right) also disappeared as the club descended down the divisions, but the Seasiders have ambitious plans for a superstadium, which rail lobbyists believed could be served by a new station. Early in 1996, however, the club announced that the new stadium was to be built on a fresh site – near the end of the M55 – but three years later, to the chagrin of supporters, it had still not materialised. *Fred Nettleton*

Right Commuter trains were often stored overnight in the station itself rather than the sidings, and the carriages had to be heated up ready for the outward journey on winter mornings. This was done by two locos at Central that never went anywhere. Parked between platforms 6 and 7, the stationary pair of former L&Y Barton Wright 0-4-4 tank engines stood bunker to bunker as carriage heating boilers with special chimney extensions. *Evening Gazette*

North Station

Below This 1932 Ordnance Survey map illustrates what was still described as the 'Poulton & Blackpool Branch'. It shows the main terminus, the excursion platforms, goods depot and yard, engine shed and carriage sidings. *Crown Copyright*

Opposite above Many overhead shots were taken of Central Station – thanks to the proximity of the Tower and the old round-the-Tower pleasure flights. Such views of North Station are rarer. This unusual aerial shot was taken from the roof of the Talbot Road car park in July 1967.

The excursion platforms, 7 to 16, are in the distance on the left of the main station. This photograph and the aerial view of the station frontage overleaf were discovered in a cupboard at the former Tyldesley School in the early 1980s. *Paul Nettleton collection*

Opposite below This second aerial view, taken from an aircraft in the 1960s, shows the extent of North's twin-arched train shed and six main platforms. The excursion platforms, the site of the present station, are off the picture to the left. Across Talbot Road is the station's great rival, the 1939 bus station and high-rise car park, from which the two other aerial shots were taken. *Evening Gazette*

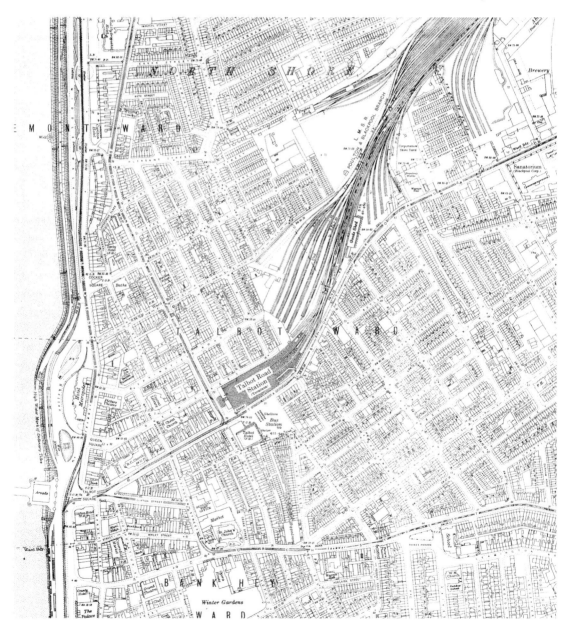

Above The imposing, though internally spartan, Ionic-style building of Talbot Road Station was the original railway gateway to Blackpool, opened in 1846 with the branch from Poulton to Blackpool. This picture is believed to have been taken just before it was replaced by a new terminus in 1898. *Evening Gazette*

Below Ninety years before the Government's White Paper on integrated transport, no fewer than five forms of travel – horse and cart, tram, rail, motor car and foot – come together in this classic view of Talbot Road Station soon after the opening of the new terminus in 1898. A horse-drawn cart heads north along Dickson Road past the Station Hotel while another waits outside the terminus. Meanwhile, further along the road, a tram trundles along on the newly launched Fleetwood-Talbot Road Station route. The young boy in knee-breeches seems to skip with excited anticipation as he approaches the station with his parents. Beneath the impressive ironwork of the station awning, an equally impressive motor car with the registration number FR 492 prepares to leave. A sign directs day-trippers up Queen Street to the excursion platforms.

Above The sprawling 1898 structure stood on the corner of Talbot Road and Dickson Road until its demolition three-quarters of a century later; from 1979 it was the site successively of no fewer than four superstores – Fine Fare, Gateway, Food Giant and the present Kwik Save. For many years around the turn of the century, a lone police constable stood on point duty before the installation of traffic lights at the busy junction. At Christmas, the officer – PC No 1, Charlie Walmsley – would receive presents from taxi drivers as a token of their appreciation of his work. *Evening Gazette*

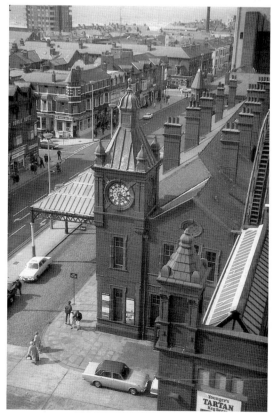

Right At precisely 4.30 in the afternoon at Blackpool North Station, passengers are thin on the ground beneath the solid, red-brick clock tower of the terminus. This picture, taken from the roof of the nearby Talbot Road car park, is undated, but can be fixed into a fairly precise timeframe – between October 1963, when the Dickson Road tram route was closed, and mid-1973, when demolition of the station began. The Triumph Herald to the right of the clock tower provides a further clue to the date. In tramway days, the Dickson Road terminus featured an automatic trolley reverser, which meant that conductors did not have to run round their vehicles with their long bamboo trolley poles. *Paul Nettleton collection*

RAILS TO BLACKPOOL

Above The cobbled parcels platform and staff car park entrance at North Station, as a Royal Mail train is unloaded during a go-slow in April 1972. *Evening Gazette*

Below Finally, by 1991, Blackpool North looked like this. The new terminus, opened in January 1974, is based on the 1938 concrete canopy covering the entrance to the excursion platforms. The once gloomy, hangar-like concourse has been brightened up by internal improvements and the addition of the triple-triangular glass awning under the £2.4 million Lancashire Lines programme between BR and Lancashire County Council. *Evening Gazette*

Above Diesels began to replace some steam trains from Blackpool to Fleetwood and Manchester with the introduction of the summer timetable on 15 June 1959. A shiny BR Derby-built two-car DMU set pulls out of Blackpool North on a trial run earlier that month. *Evening Gazette*

Below Almost 25 years later, in a picture taken from a virtually identical angle to the 1896 photograph on page 18, a now ageing three-car DMU leaves Blackpool North for Manchester Victoria in July 1983. On the left are the truncated tracks that led to the original terminus in Talbot Road. The land is now occupied by a station car park, cab rank and superstore. *British Railways*

Left The old timber Blackpool North No 1 signal box with, immediately behind it, the brick-built replacement, which still stands near Devonshire Road bridge. The picture was taken in May 1965 during the last few days in which the old L&Y box was in operation before its successor took over. Blackpool North is the biggest British terminus still to be controlled exclusively by mechanical signalling. No 1 box controls the northerly end of the carriage sidings, while the larger No 2 cabin – dating back to 1896 – controls the station and the southern end of the sidings, which latterly became a dumping-ground for rakes of obsolete DMUs and EMUs. It boasts a sign familiar to millions of expectant visitors: 'Blackpool North – 300 yards'. No 2 box originally had 120 levers, but today less than half remain. Before 1973 there was a third box, covering the original station in Dickson Road. *J. B. Hodgson collection, Lancashire & Yorkshire Railway Society*

Below No 1 times two! A side-on view of the old and new Blackpool No 1 signal boxes. With the prospect of resignalling of the line in the new Millennium, there was speculation that No 1 box might become the only one at North Station. If that were to happen, both Blackpool Civic Trust and Blackpool & Fylde Rail Users' Association said they would press for the former L&Y No 2 box to be designated as a listed building because of its historical value. *Fred Worman*

A signalman at work inside No 1 box, with some of the 52 levers in operation in July 1932. A visiting *Gazette* journalist in the same year described how peak-period trains left every 5 minutes into the small hours – to London, Lichfield or Leamington. 'It will be almost four o'clock when the last train gets out, and the first in is due soon after five.' *Evening Gazette*

On the centenary of Blackpool North No 2 signal box in 1996, the author, with Malcolm Richardson of Blackpool & Fylde Rail Users' Association and Barry Shaw from Blackpool Civic Trust, was given a glimpse behind the scenes of the historic structure. The April visit was arranged by Railtrack's Ray Browell. *Malcolm Richardson*

RAILS TO BLACKPOOL

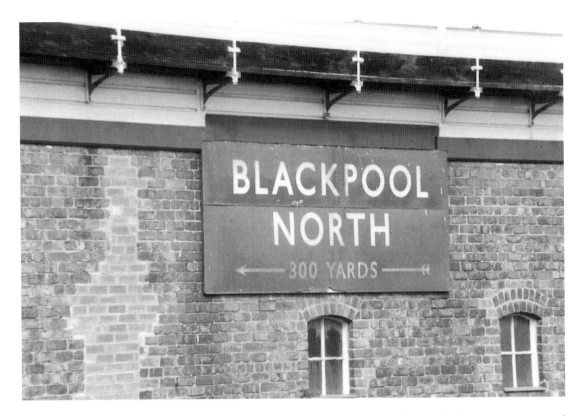

Above The famous maroon enamel plate on the side of No 2 signal box declares 'Blackpool North – 300 yards'. The box had been built in 1896 as part of the construction of the new Talbot Road station, which opened two years later. *Malcolm Richardson*

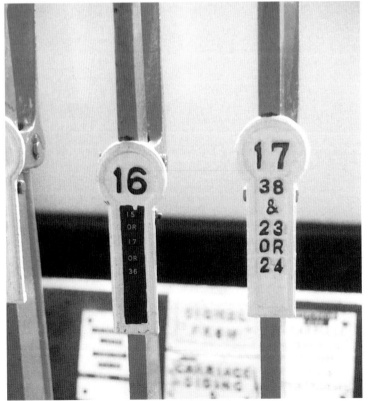

Left Despite the removal of many of the levers, No 2 remained a busy box, controlling signals and carriage sidings. Two of the freshly painted red signal levers, with their black-on-white number panels, are seen in this close-up of part of the lever frame. *Barry Shaw*

RAILWAYS OF BLACKPOOL AND THE FYLDE

Right The old and the new at Blackpool North shed in the mid-1960s. English Electric Type 4 diesel-electric No D209 is pictured alongside 'Black Five' No 45131. The sheer statistics of the shed in its heyday were mind-boggling; an *Evening Gazette* reporter invited into North shed late one Illuminations Saturday in 1932 observed a pile of 5,000 tons of coal 8 feet high stretching down one side of the building. About 75 engines were compressed into an area 500 yards by 100, and a really thirsty loco could take 3,000 gallons of water in one draught: 'There is a great deal of humanity about these engines'. *Fred Nettleton*

Middle right Regular Pullmans pulled into Blackpool for the first time in May 1986 when BR unveiled the coaches and top-class service standards that were to be the hallmark of its new luxury express to London. The Mayor and Mayoress of Blackpool, Councillor and Mrs Tony Battersby, and local MP Norman Miscampbell joined business leaders on a special preview run of the 'Lancashire Pullman' to Crewe and back. However, the service was to be one of the casualties of InterCity's withdrawal from Blackpool in September 1992. The 1st Class Pullman carriage *Sir John Barbirolli* is in the forefront as VIPs prepare to board the train for the preview visit. *Evening Gazette*

Right Even the diminutive Class '02' Yorkshire Engine Co 0-4-0 diesel No D2863 towers above these two shunters, complete with their poles, in Blackpool North goods yard *circa* 1964. The driver is Albert Durant, and the shunters Ron Singleton (left) and Malcolm Handforth. *Don Rutter*

Above The magnificent double arch of the 1898 North Station train shed in May 1973, soon after demolition of the terminus began. As the breakers move in, the track has already been lifted and much of the platform area filled in. *Evening Gazette*

Below These two weighty and rusting cast-iron plaques bearing the monograms of the L&Y and LNWR – who jointly ran the station until their merger on 1 January 1922, a year ahead of the national Grouping – had stood at North Station's entrance since it was rebuilt in 1898. They were displayed at the entrance to Fine Fare when it opened in 1979, but wind, salt and sand took their toll, and they were restored to their former glory by Blackpool Civic Trust and today occupy pride of place inside what is now the Kwik Save store. Transport writer Graham Twidale, helped by colleague Harold Hodgson, had the logos sandblasted by Interblast, and enlisted Blackpool Transport signwriter Bryan Hamer to paint the intricate emblems. Trust Chairman Barry Shaw said, 'They have been around for almost 100 years and now they will last another 100.' The pristine plaques were unveiled by the Civic Trust as part of British Telecom Environment Week in 1993. Meanwhile, in the 1993 North West Best Kept Station awards, Blackpool North won the Regional Railways NW Best Major Station prize and also the Best Major Station accolade in the PSO – Public Service Obligation grant – category. *Barry Shaw*

South Station

The changing face of South Station. 'Black Five' No 44950 passes beneath the footbridge on platform 1 in May 1968 – the last spring of steam. By the mid-1980s, however, the bridge had gone and the station had been reduced to a shadow of its former self: a single, unstaffed platform. The footpath leading to the bridge alongside an immaculately tended garden had also vanished, as had the signal box that stood at the end of the platform. But the second picture, taken from a similar angle on 3 July 1993, shows the service to be better patronised than the nearby car park, as a Class 142 'Pacer' unit stands at the former platform 1 on the coastal side of the station. Fears remain that the line could eventually be truncated at Burlington Road, though Blackpool Council, Labour-controlled since 1991, has demonstrated its commitment to rail by a suggested tram-train interchange at the Pleasure Beach Station. *Evening Gazette/Paul Nettleton*

This spectacular aerial shot from 1964 shows Blackpool South Station in its prime, though even then the writing was on the wall. Originally Waterloo Road, in 1916 it was converted into a junction station for the new Marton Line, with an island platform to serve the coast line; it was renamed Blackpool South on 17 March 1932. The Marton Line forks to the right and the coastal route to Lytham is seen heading away to the left; carriage sidings lay in the fork of the 'Y'. The Marton Line was used only sporadically in the two years before its closure in 1967; just one scheduled train a day ran on it in 1966. Today the former railway land is occupied by, among others, superstores and a family pub. *Evening Gazette*

RAILWAYS OF BLACKPOOL AND THE FYLDE

Above Blackpool Central's loco-servicing facilities were under such pressure that a second turntable was installed opposite Seymour Road, in the sidings between Bloomfield Road and South Station, to supplement them. Here, 'Black Five' 4-6-0 No 44692 stands near the water tower some time in the 1950s. Partially in view is a Class '4MT' 2-6-4T.

Below The last steam-hauled Preston to Blackpool train ran on 3 August 1968 – the eve of the final day of scheduled main-line steam on BR – in the shape of 'Black Five' No 45212. The loco, which attracted legions of enthusiasts to Blackpool South Station, is now preserved on the Keighley & Worth Valley Railway. On board was one of a long line of ecclesiastical railway enthusiasts, the Reverend David Scotland, minister of Blackpool's Claremont United Reformed Church from 1963 to 1970, who died in 1993 aged 82. *Evening Gazette*

Above The symbolism is hard to escape in this view from the early years of the 20th century. A new-fangled motor car, occupied by broad-brim-bonneted ladies, passes over the skew bridge in Lytham Road, obliterating part of the old South Shore Station building. This was once the only intermediate stopping-point on the Blackpool & Lytham Railway, and its largely timber station was served by the trams of both the Blackpool and Lytham St Annes operations until its closure in 1916, when Waterloo Road, the new junction station at the intersection with the Marton Line, rendered it redundant. In this view, looking north along the tram lines towards the Tower, two trams pass as horse-drawn cabs wait outside the station, and the covered ramp down to the platforms is clearly visible. After its closure, the station building was shifted bodily to a new location a mile eastwards – as two semi-detached houses in Rough Heys Lane, Marton Moss, complete with the tall and distinctive L&Y chimney.

Left Visitors travelling on the coastal line to Blackpool South today are left in no doubt that they are entering a holiday resort, as the track borders the white-knuckle rides of the Pleasure Beach. Here in 1994 a Class 142 'Pacer' unit cannot match the G-forces of the 85 mph, 235-foot Pepsi Max Big One roller-coaster that dominates the background. *Paul Nettleton*

2.
FYLDE MISCELLANY

Below left Blackpool traffic was not all one-way. Out of season, as well as the daily commuter and club trains to the big commercial centres of east Lancashire, Manchester and Liverpool, there were excursions to places of interest in Yorkshire, Cumbria, Derbyshire and beyond. Football fans could travel from Blackpool Central to the FA Cup 4th Round tie between the Seasiders and Blackburn Rovers in January 1960 for 4s 3d. Today much of the line between these two great Lancashire towns has been reduced to a single-track branch.

This BR bill advertises Sunday special excursions from Blackpool via the coastal line to Chesterfield and Barrow-in-Furness, via Carnforth, on the former Furness Railway. Carnforth was the location of the now closed Steamtown railway museum, where some of the locos that once served the Fylde were preserved. *Fred Nettleton collection*

Below right Nice train, shame about the station… At the Blackpool boundary on the coastal line lies SQUIRES GATE, with a Class 153 diesel unit stopping at the run-down station in 1995. Daubed with graffiti and vandalised,

it was the only Fylde station not to be improved under the Lancashire Lines modernisation programme. In 1996, however, Railtrack finally upgraded the station as part of a five-year modernisation programme in the North West.

The station is sandwiched between two significant potential markets, Pontin's holiday centre to the left and the airport to the right. Rail and air transport have always co-existed closely in Blackpool. In 1910 the pioneer aviator A. V. Roe – founder of Avro – transported two aircraft from Brooklands in Surrey to Blackpool by train for one of the town's early air shows. As the engine struggled up an incline near Wigan, however, sparks from the loco set both machines alight.

Ambitious wartime plans for the expansion of the airport into a huge international terminal, catering for 50,000 passengers a day, never materialised; nor did later suggestions for a plane-train interchange at Squires Gate. Now the remains of the sidings that linked the railway to the huge wartime aircraft manufacturing hangars are barely visible on the industrial estate that occupies much of the site. *Paul Nettleton*

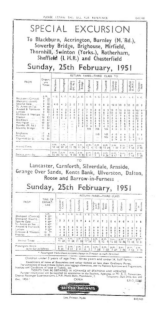

Above This was the handsome frontage of Squires Gate Station soon after its opening on 14 September 1931. It was a belated replacement for the short-lived Stony Hill Station, which was open from April 1865 to September 1872. The LMS originally shared the premises with a bank; the sturdy structure's booking office, now demolished, was at street level, with steps leading down from the road bridge to the two platforms. The following June, the Earl of Plymouth, Parliamentary Under-Secretary at the Ministry of Transport, opened the new bridge on which the station stood – a ceremony marked by a plaque on the parapet. *Evening Gazette*

Below Ground-level halts were opened on the South Fylde line at GILLETT'S CROSSING, between St Annes and Blackpool near the Old Links golf course, and at Burlington Road, South Shore, on 1 October 1913. They closed exactly two years later but reopened on 1 March 1920, before final closure on 11 September 1939. In this picture from about 1924, ex-L&Y 0-4-0 steam railmotor No 10607, on a Blackpool Central to Lytham service, stops at Gillett's Crossing. It was named after nearby Gillett's Farm: sparks from steam locos could set surrounding agricultural land on fire, which led to exchanges of correspondence between landowners and the railway. *Evening Gazette*

RAILWAYS OF BLACKPOOL AND THE FYLDE

Above Five faces of ST ANNES Station, showing how it has been transformed over the course of a century. In the first, with the landau outside – perhaps waiting to take a visiting family to their lodgings – the old half-timbered station looks more like a country house than a Victorian railway building. It opened as Cross Slack on the Blackpool & Lytham in 1870, but was replaced by a second station three years later, and was renamed St Annes-on-the-Sea in January 1875. *Evening Gazette*

Below The graceful approach to St Annes Station in 1906. The entrance to the station is to the left, while the road to the right – The Crescent – rises to the bridge that crosses the railway line. Not a car is in sight. *Commercial postcard*

The original station was replaced in 1926 by a grander affair. The attractive awning shields a two-car DMU en route to Blackpool South in October 1984, shortly before demolition of the seaward-side platform buildings (left) to make way for a supermarket and new booking office. *Lytham St Annes Express*

The photograph above shows demolition work in progress in 1985. The substantial buildings on the landward platform also fell into decay after closure, and in 1995 workmen demolished that once-imposing structure too – including the impressive wrought-iron canopy – by hand to ensure no damage was caused to the track and neighbouring properties. Fylde Council had threatened to prosecute BR unless the buildings were demolished.

The remaining single track is served by a compact but well-designed brick booking office and waiting room, which features photographs of the line in its prime. In late 1998 the supermarket group Safeway announced plans to replace its store in St Annes, which would involve demolishing the station building and relocating it near the wooded embankment by The Crescent. Blackpool & Fylde Rail Users' Association Chairman Paul Nettleton stressed that any replacement station must be at least on a par with the existing structure, which was the best-used intermediate station on the line. And he suggested that Safeway, which had already begun using rail to transport some of its products, could open a private siding in St Annes. *Paul Nettleton/Evening Gazette*

Left A run-down ANSDELL & FAIRHAVEN Station in 1975. The station buildings have now been demolished, though the steep steps to the island platforms have been supplemented by a new access ramp for disabled people. The station opened in 1872 and was replaced by a second building 300 metres to the west on 10 October 1903. Even a relatively small station had its own goods facilities, seen through the bridge towards Lytham. *Evening Gazette*

Below Wintry woods: a 30-year-old DMU heads through snow-flecked Witch Wood at Ansdell early in 1990. The elderly units had reappeared to counter a desperate shortage of rolling-stock. The woodland walk between Ansdell and Lytham stations was officially opened by the Duke of Edinburgh in 1985. It is hard to believe that this deceptively rural setting is barely 5 miles from the bustle of central Blackpool. *Paul Nettleton*

Elegant LYTHAM Station (*above*) in 1931, one of the finely detailed drawings by the late Mr Frank Dickinson that were reproduced as postcards in 1984.

The station still stands (*below*), but the classical-style building has now been converted into a pub-restaurant after declining into a virtual ruin. The attraction, built sympathetically into the shell of the station building, was opened in a £600,000 joint venture between Fylde Council and the private sector. The former railmotor bay, to the left of the footbridge in this 1989 shot, now forms part of a car park. *Lytham St Annes Heritage Card Collection/Evening Gazette*

Left This 1860s Ordnance Survey map of the South Fylde area shows the astonishing absence of any link between the two lines serving Lytham. The terminus of the Blackpool & Lytham Railway, which opened in 1863, was several hundred yards from its counterpart on the 1846 branch from the Preston & Wyre. However, after the line was taken over by the L&Y and LNWR, in 1874 the two routes were connected and the original Lytham terminus was closed, becoming a goods station. On the map, St Annes does not yet exist. The former spur to Lytham Dock – one of the principal reasons for the original decision to build the line from Kirkham – branches off to the south of Moss Side Station. *Crown Copyright*

Below By the time this 1911 Ordnance Survey map was published, the 'Lytham link' between the two stations had been put in place. The former P&W terminus had been converted into a goods station and yard, and is today the site of the town's fire station. The connection with the Blackpool and Lytham line had been made and the L&Y/LNWR joint station was on its present site on the far left of the picture, off Ballam Road. Note the intensive housing development that has taken place in the half century between the publication of the two maps. The former Lytham St Annes tramway – a response to the residential development, and initially operated by gas-powered vehicles – ran along Clifton Street and Warton Street, with the tramshed off Henry Street. *Crown Copyright*

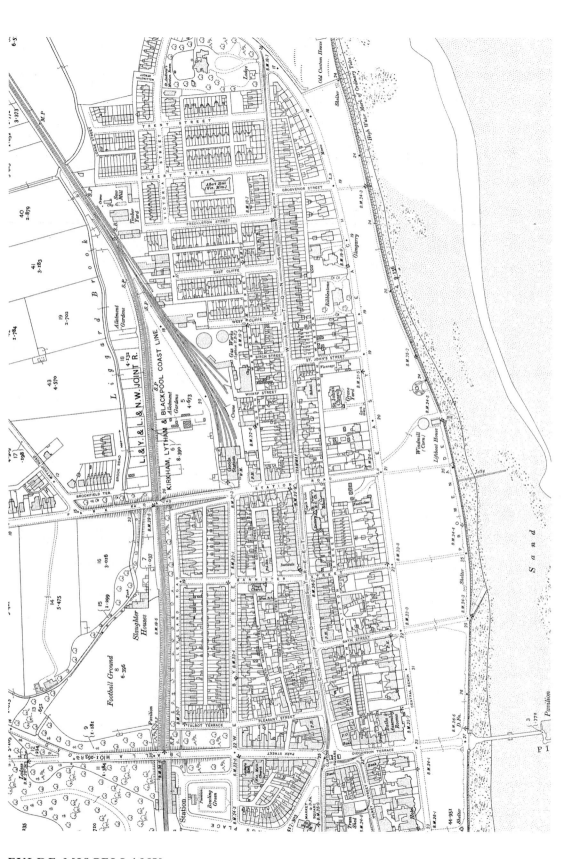

Above MOSS SIDE Station, north-east of Lytham, dating back to 1846, was closed on 26 June 1961 at the same time as its contemporary and neighbour, Wrea Green. It catered for a diverse range of passengers – from relatives visiting the now-closed Moss Side Hospital to farmers making early-morning milk deliveries to the dairy in St Annes. The former signal box and the manual level-crossing gates it controlled are seen with the overgrown platforms in this 1982 picture looking towards Kirkham. The cabin closed in 1983 when the down line between Lytham and Kirkham was lifted. *Evening Gazette*

Below On 21 November 1983, however, the station reopened, with Lancashire County Council footing most of the bill for the single unmanned platform. This was coupled with the introduction of a new half-barrier automatic level crossing. The County Council and Wrea Green residents are also pressing for the reopening of the latter village's own halt on a similar basis.

The line between Lytham and Moss Side witnessed the Fylde's worst railway disaster on 3 November 1924, when the 4.40 pm 'businessmen's express' from Liverpool to Blackpool Central left the rails near Warton Crossing. The driver and 12 passengers died and 35 people were injured. A Ministry of Transport inquiry concluded that the crash was caused by failure of a tyre on the 4-4-0 engine. *Paul Nettleton*

Above From February 1846 to November 1853, about three-quarters of a mile to the west of the current Kirkham Junction, stood Lytham Junction Station, at the original sharp intersection of the P&W Lytham branch with the main line; a new, more direct cut-off to Wrea Green was opened in 1874, bypassing the former acute junction. War Department 'Austerity' 2-8-0 No 90271, based at Fleetwood, steams west from Kirkham with an excursion for Blackpool Central in July 1959. *Jack Fenton*

Below The king-size KIRKHAM NORTH JUNCTION signal box, which had 75 levers, still dominates the much-reduced trackwork outside the town's station. The box opened in 1903 with the new Marton Line to Blackpool. Officially known simply as 'Kirkham' after 1975, it still had its former full title on its nameboard. The absence of any trains is explained by the fact that the picture was taken in August 1994 during a 24-hour signalmen's strike. Weeds have reclaimed much of the marshalling yards at what was once one of Britain's busiest provincial junctions. The earthworks that led to the spectacular single-track flyover for trains on the Marton Line from Blackpool Central are still visible behind the box, but only an abutment remains of the bridge itself. *Evening Gazette*

Above A view of Kirkham North Junction in April 1972. The coastal line can be seen branching off to the left, and the former flying junction carrying the up Marton Line over the Fleetwood route is visible in the distance, but the track has been lifted. A three-car DMU heads for Blackpool North while red flags indicate the closure of the down fast line; some of the signal arms and crossovers have also been removed. *Jack Fenton*

Below In full flight at KIRKHAM & WESHAM in August 1966, 'Jubilee' Class 4-6-0 No 45694 *Bellerophon* – a Fylde Coast favourite – makes a stirring sight with its trail of exhaust as it nears the water column, on the extreme right, next to the section of quadruple track outside Kirkham & Wesham Station. *Jack Fenton*

Above KIRKHAM & WESHAM Station: 'Black Five' No 44667 heads light for Preston sheds on 27 March 1967. On the right is Kirkham Station box, which has now been demolished following closure in 1975; Kirkham South box was taken out of use in 1969. *Locofotos*

Below Twenty-five years later, in 1992, a Class 37 diesel-electric with a club train bound for Blackpool North leaves Kirkham. The cobbles lead to the former goods yard, and the top of the refurbished station building, at road level with steps down to the island platforms, is just visible in the background. Information services and the booking office were moved up to street level in a £100,000 facelift. On 15 July 1990 a plaque to mark the 150th anniversary of the P&W was unveiled at the station by Alderman George Bamber, himself a former railwayman.

To the north-west of Kirkham lay Weeton signal box (where there had also briefly been a halt in the early 1840s) and the station and cabin at Singleton, which until its demolition was the oldest and smallest of the L&Y boxes on the line. Like Weeton's, it was built by Saxby & Farmer. The station, some distance from the village it served, opened in 1870 and closed on 2 May 1932; no trace of it remains. On 16 July 1961 seven people were killed and 116 injured when a six-car DMU taking trippers from Colne to Fleetwood and the Isle of Man ferry hit a stationary ballast train on Singleton Bank. *Paul Nettleton*

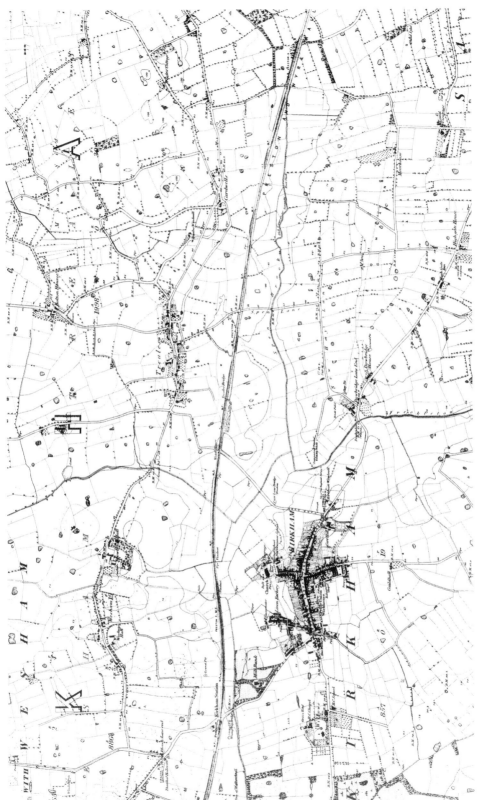

The route of the railway through Kirkham has lain virtually unchanged since this 1844 Ordnance Survey map, just four years after the Preston & Wyre opened and two years before the branch to Lytham began operation. Kirkham Station (north-west of the town) was originally located to the west of the road, but was moved to the east during the redevelopment of 1889–90. As can be seen, the station was some distance from the centre of the town and was, in fact, in the neighbouring settlement of Wesham. (This was reflected in the renaming of the station as Kirkham & Wesham in the early 1900s.) The population of Kirkham in the 1851 census was no more than 2,799, although the market town was already an important textiles centre, as the linen factory (between town centre and station) demonstrates.

Further to the east (two-thirds of the way along the line in the second map) is Lea Road Station; Salwick had not yet opened. Note the meandering route of the railway's predecessor and partial rival, the Lancaster Canal, which from Salwick runs roughly parallel with the P&W. Winding through the sparsely populated countryside to the south-east of Kirkham is the toll road that was the main means of transport between Preston and Kirkham before the arrival of the railway. This 6-inches-to-the-mile map is based on a survey by Captain Tucker and Lieutenants Hamley and Stanley of the Royal Engineers. *Crown Copyright*

Above A track-level view of 'Black Five' 4-6-0 No 45227 as it speeds through LAYTON past a lineside hut near Crossley's Bridge at the head of a parcels train from Blackpool North in September 1966. *Fred Nettleton*

Left Taken from the footbridge, this shot shows another 'Black Five', No 45072, arriving at Layton Station on a Bradford to Blackpool North service on 12 August 1967. The station opened as Bispham in May 1867, being renamed Layton on 4 July 1938. *Fred Nettleton*

Left Signalman Mr Ian Lyons takes a brief break from duties at the old brick and timber Layton box in August 1967. In July 1998 Mr Lyons, who had started his career as an apprentice signalman at Sowerby Bridge, retired from Blackpool No 2 box after 45 years on the railway following his 60th birthday. He had moved to the Fylde in 1961 to take up the signalman's job at Poulton. Layton box is now long-gone, but to the east the handsomely repainted Carleton Crossing cabin, built to an LNWR pattern, controls the only level crossing on the Blackpool North route. *Fred Nettleton*

Above An elegiac view of 'Cleveley' Station, THORNTON, in the early 1900s as two passengers stare intently at the camera in the signal box. On the opposite platform a four-coach push-pull service arrives from Poulton en route to Fleetwood, hauled by an L&Y 2-4-2T. The story of Thornton Station is a thorny one: it boasted no fewer than five names in its 130-year history. Ramper Road Station (soon renamed simply Ramper) survived barely a year after its opening on the P&W line in 1842. A new station – Cleveleys – was opened near the site of the old halt in 1865, though some 2 miles from the small resort after which it was named. The station was to the south of the level crossing; immediately to the north of the road stood a squat signal box. On 1 April 1905, it was renamed Thornton for Cleveleys, but in 1925 was succeeded by a third station, located to the north of the level crossing. In a 1913 holiday guide, the L&Y advised tourists heading to Thornton for Cleveleys to send their luggage in advance. Passenger services to Thornton were withdrawn on 1 June 1970, the station buildings and signal box were demolished and the land used for a supermarket. The derelict platforms of the station, which had again been renamed – Thornton – in February 1953, are still clearly visible from Victoria Road East. A similar fate befell Burn Naze Station to the north, where trains first stopped on 12 October 1908.

Below Preston-based ex-LNWR 'G2' – later LMS Class '7F' – 0-8-0 freight loco No 49024 brings what little road traffic there is to a halt at Thornton level crossing in the early 1950s. By then the station had been moved to the right of the crossing. Meanwhile anyone dreaming of a real-life home on the rails could have had their wish fulfilled after British Rail decided in 1995 to sell the former cottage of the Hillylaid crossing keeper in Lawsons Road, Thornton. The level crossing still lies outside the front door of the picturesque, brick-built cottage, which dates back to the early days of the P&W. *Evening Gazette*

Generations of eager children have played the game of 'spot the Tower' as they have headed by rail to Blackpool across the pancake-flat panorama of the Fylde plain. But passengers travelling to Europe's biggest holiday resort can also see some other towers – smaller, perhaps, but almost as magnificent in their grace and grandeur. In Victorian times a dozen windmills could be seen from the railway routes into the Fylde, and for one small boy from industrial Bolton, the first sight of the Fylde's windmills from a carriage window led to a lifelong fascination.

Allen Clarke, author, political polemicist, sociologist, cyclist, countryman, poet and publisher, immortalised the area in his classic book *Windmill Land*. His love of the Fylde had been inspired by a visit to Blackpool he made from smoky Bolton, where he had worked in the mills as an 11-year-old. In his book he recalls that he was so excited by the prospect of the trip – which left before dawn – that he put his trousers on back to front.

Clarke was self-taught and a stalwart socialist. His life was transformed when he won a scholarship to Hulton Grammar School in Bolton, and by the age of 15 he was a pupil teacher. Clarke and his wife, Lila, became so enraptured by the Fylde on their visits to the coast that they decided to settle in the area. They would explore its lanes by bicycle, and the result was his heartfelt tribute to a pre-industrial lifestyle that was already disappearing even as he wrote.

His love of the windmills had been nurtured by that train trip to Blackpool one Whitsuntide. In an article for the *Blackpool Gazette & Herald*, submitted shortly before he died in 1935 aged 72 and published after his death, he recalled the discomfort of the Victorian 'cheap trips' to the resort. The fare was half a crown (2s 6d), and the train accommodation crude and primitive, with hard, cushionless carriages. 'Indeed, sometimes cattle trucks were cleaned and fitted up with a few seats for cheap excursions... What a delightful transformation in the matter of comfort are the railway coaches of today!'

However, his most profound memory of that day trip was a sight witnessed a full 15 miles before his train pulled into Talbot Road. It was the windmill in Treales, between Preston and Kirkham (now a private residence), which for the youthful Clarke would develop into the repository of a potent blend of literary and political associations. For Clarke, the windmills symbolised a more civilised, natural and romantic means of production that preceded the grimness and the grime of the Industrial Revolution.

In an introduction to the 1986 facsimile edition of *Windmill Land*, Dr Paul Salveson, Director of the Transport Research & Information Network (TR&IN), echoed that first journey made by Clarke to the Fylde Coast.

'If you ask anyone brought up in the Lancashire cotton towns what their first memories of childhood were – happy ones, at any rate – the chances are they'll tell you it was getting on the train and setting off for Blackpool.'

The rail approaches to Fleetwood were dominated by the towering presence of the mill seen here, Marsh Mill at Thornton, the tallest in the Fylde, rising to six storeys. It was built by the uncle of railway pioneer Sir Peter Hesketh Fleetwood in 1794 and is now the heart of a Wyre Council craft, heritage and leisure centre. It is pictured in Edwardian times in a painting by the late John Green of Marton, the former chairman of Blackpool Civic Trust.

Right The West Coast Main Line skirts the eastern fringe of the Fylde, taking in the former Lancaster & Preston Junction Railway, which was officially opened on 25 June 1840. It shared the level corridor between the Fylde and the Bowland Fells with its two rivals, the turnpike road and the Lancaster Canal. The stunning spire of St Walburge's Church in PRESTON marks Maudlands Junction, where the Fylde lines meet the West Coast route; sleeper blocks from the L&PJR were used in the construction of the spire. Here, a train in the charge of 'Black Five' No 44982 approaches Preston Station from the Blackpool tracks in August 1965. *Locofotos*

Below Almost midway between Preston and Lancaster was GARSTANG & CATTERALL Station, dating back to the opening of the L&PJR and some distance from Garstang itself and the Knott End railway's Garstang Town Station. When the Garstang & Knott End Railway opened in 1870, its trains used the west side of the down island platform. The attractive building on the up platform is seen here on 12 August 1967, 18 months before the station's closure, with the signal box visible through the footbridge.

From the road below, the station looked even more imposing, with its nine arches and steep steps to the platform. To the south, looking from the footbridge towards Preston (*below*), lay the station's small goods yard. Following closure the Garstang & District Rail Action Group launched a campaign for restoration of a station serving the market town, but in 1998 county councillors said that it would have to be considered as part of their new local transport plan.

Further south still, the former Broughton Station at Crow Hall was moved to School Lane in 1840 and renamed Barton & Broughton in April 1861. With Brock, Scorton and Galgate, the station lasted until 1 May 1939. However, nearby Roebuck had disappeared from the timetable as early as August 1849. Another of the original 1840 stations named after a coaching inn, Bay Horse, serving the villages of Forton and Cockerham, remained open until 13 June 1960. *All F. W. Shuttleworth*

3.
FLEETWOOD

Trains, trams and trawlers

Fleetwood was perhaps the first 'new town' in the world to be created by the railway, developed by the enlightened Lord of the Manor, Sir Peter Hesketh Fleetwood. The decision to push a railway out to a windswept wilderness on the north-west of the Fylde peninsula, described in contemporary reports as a barren rabbit warren, was bold and visionary, and inspired the creation of a port and resort that was a model for similar ventures across Britain.

The Preston & Wyre Railway Act received the Royal Assent on 3 July 1835, authorising a capital of £130,000 and giving powers to construct a line from a terminus at Maudlands, Preston, to the mouth of the River Wyre. Building began in May 1836 with George Staunton as contractor; an additional contract for a 2-mile embankment at Burn Naze was awarded in May 1839. In the same year George and Robert Stephenson were appointed

Victor's laurels: a bewhiskered Sir Peter Hesketh Fleetwood, with his patrician good looks, powerful Roman nose and firmly chiselled chin.

engineers to complete the work. High tides delayed the construction of the embankment, despite the use of thousands of tons of rubble and stone, so a temporary timber viaduct was substituted for part of the distance.

A single line formally opened on 15 July 1840 from Maudlands, crossing the Lancaster & Preston Junction Railway on the level; there was also a connection with the North Union Station at Preston. Stations were opened at Kirkham and Poulton, and later at Lea Road and Salwick.

Kathleen Eyre, who died in 1985 after establishing an unrivalled reputation as the Fylde's foremost local historian of her day, graphically describes the tumultuous scenes surrounding the opening of the line. In her classic book *Seven Golden Miles*, she tells how a special decorated double-headed train, festooned with flags and laden with well-wishers and local worthies, left Preston (50 minutes late) and proceeded majestically towards the coast.

'From every church tower, from every house of consequence, flags flapped at full mast and cottage doorways were crammed with excited spectators. There were similar lively scenes at Poulton, and a discharge of artillery greeted the train at Fleetwood where three steamers were waiting to take the guests on a short cruise round the lighthouse.'

Afterwards the company ascended the Mount to view Sir Peter Hesketh Fleetwood's new town rising from this ostensibly inhospitable corner of north-west Lancashire. The main line of the P&W was doubled between 1846 and 1851.

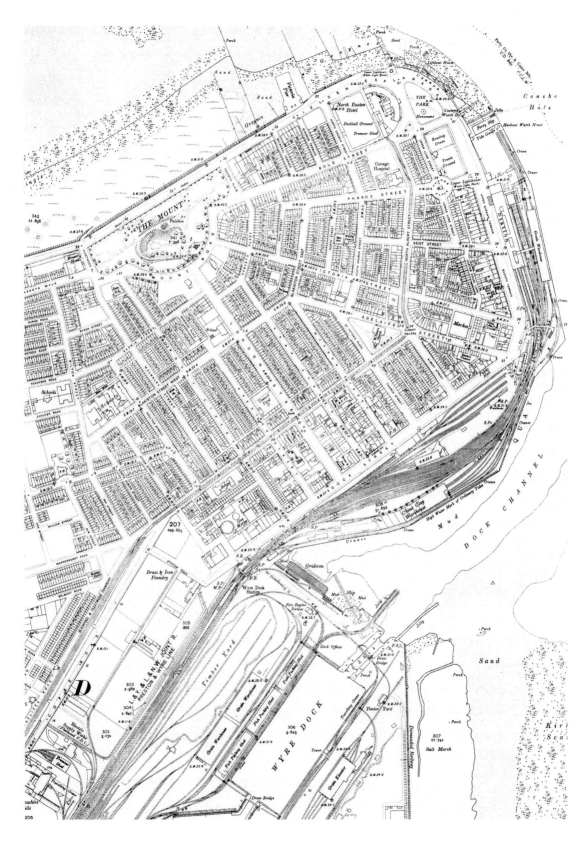

RAILWAYS OF BLACKPOOL AND THE FYLDE

Left This Ordnance Survey map published in 1912 shows just how significant the railway was in Fleetwood's formation. By that date the port's population was approaching 15,000, and had increased more than fivefold since the 1841 Census. An entire section of the map is dominated by a complex configuration of parallel railway lines, snaking around the coastal contours of the Wyre estuary. Still visible (bottom right) are the remains of the original P&W line (marked 'Dismantled Railway'); the precarious embankment across the part of the estuary known as Cold Dubbs was replaced in February 1851 by the line hugging the coast to the west.

The abandonment of the embankment allowed some of the land on the inner side to be reclaimed for development, including the opening in October 1877 of a new docks complex. Covering 10 acres, it had 2,700 feet of quay space and was served by more than 8 miles of railway line, with two tracks completely encircling the docks – an outstanding example of an intricate, interlinking infrastructure between rail and sea transport. It was designed to make the transfer of goods from trawler to train as smooth as possible. There was also a substantial timber pond with its own rail sidings. In 1883 the Lancashire & Yorkshire Railway further extended the docks with a grain elevator that could load cargoes at the rate of 120 tons an hour.

By the outbreak of the First World War more than 50,000 tons of fish a year were being landed, and about 100 steam trawlers were based in the port. From the dockside the railway line ran north-east alongside Dock Street, where the original 1840 P&W terminus stood opposite the Crown Hotel. *Crown Copyright*

Above On 15 July 1883 the austerely imposing new terminus was opened next to the steamer berths at a cost of £120,000. The Dock Street terminus was closed and another new station, Wyre Dock, opened on 1 December 1885. The new station opposite Queens Terrace allowed passengers to step straight from their train across the platform, under cover throughout, to one of the ferries operated by the North Lancashire Steam Navigation Company. This LNWR postcard shows the steamer *Duke of Connaught* plying between Fleetwood and Belfast in 1904.

Below Passengers who sought a less hectic changeover could book into the North Euston. The hotel's name harked back to early hopes that the line would form part of the main West Coast route to Scotland, and it contained baths, an ice-house and even its own private pier. However, the construction of a line over Shap Fell in 1848 rendered the Fleetwood route to Scotland, connecting to Ardrossan by ferry, obsolete. The North Euston retained its name but lost its grand role, if not its architectural grandeur. The graceful curve of the hotel is seen here from the beach in this postcard view from the summer of 1912.

North Euston Hotel, Fleetwood.

786

Above A closer glimpse of the hotel's sturdy, substantial architecture and classical-style portico early in the 20th century. The station is on the extreme left with the Pharos lighthouse in between.

Below The spacious and solidly constructed quayside station building and train shed at Queen's Terrace, Fleetwood, again from a turn-of-the century commercial postcard. On the far left is the funnel of one of the vessels moored at the steamer berth alongside the terminus.

The Station, Fleetwood.

RAILWAYS OF BLACKPOOL AND THE FYLDE

Above The Pharos lighthouse is just visible in the background to the left of this view of the train shed and platforms on 27 September 1958. *J. A. Peden*

Below It is exactly 3 pm in the entrance hall of Fleetwood station, with its magnificent floral displays; note the perambulator on the right. *J. A. Peden collection*

FLEETWOOD

Platform 4 from the 'business' end, looking towards the exit barriers, and *below* Horwich-type 0-4-0 steam railmotor No 12, built in 1907, preparing to leave on the shuttle to Blackpool North. *Both J. A. Peden collection*

An array of former L&Y signals stands sentinel next to Fleetwood Station box on 27 August 1955. *F. W. Shuttleworth*

Ivatt '2MT' 2-6-2T No 41283, push-pull fitted, draws out of the station in February 1959. The footbridge can also be seen in the background of the picture above. *Jack Fenton*

Left The proximity of the station to the estuary can be seen in this 1956 shot of '4MT' 2-6-4T No 42643 pulling out of the terminus with a stopping train to Manchester. The signal box is partly obscured by steam and smoke. *Locofotos*

Below At 8.56 pm on 1 November 1964 – the same day as the closure of Blackpool Central – the final Fleetwood to Blackpool North train pulled out of the port with two passengers on board. The train, manned by Fleetwood-based driver Jack Fletcher and guard Thomas Yates, was the last through service between the two towns after 65 years of operation. Less than 18 months later the quayside Fleetwood station was closed, and on 18 April 1966 a rebuilt Wyre Dock became the new terminus. The Queens Terrace station was finally demolished in 1969, although its vast expanse can still be clearly traced on the landscape, and the passenger service to Poulton was withdrawn on 1 June 1970. Like the closure of Blackpool Central, this was not one of the proposals in Dr Beeching's report on the reshaping of BR: the document had recommended the retention of the Poulton-Fleetwood link and the closure of Poulton-Blackpool North. Here enthusiasts gather at Wyre Dock Station (renamed Fleetwood) as one of the last BR steam locos, 'Black Five' No 45156 *Ayrshire Yeomanry*, visits the port in 1968. Now, the group RailRoad – brainchild of local railwayman Graham Robinson of the RMT Union – is campaigning for restoration of a rail link to Fleetwood to capitalise on the revival of freight traffic in Britain. *Evening Gazette*

RAILWAYS OF BLACKPOOL AND THE FYLDE

4.
POULTON-LE-FYLDE

Beyond the hurly-burly of Blackpool, even a tranquil market town like Poulton-le-Fylde was moulded by the railway. As the accompanying Ordnance Survey map of 1912 graphically illustrates, the railway cut several swathes through the town. In essence, there were two intersecting triangles: one, to the north-east of the town, charted the original 1840 railway and its Blackpool branch; the other, to the west, formed the new alignment and included the later station, which opened on 29 March 1896. (Its centenary coincided with the Blackpool Rail 150 celebrations.) The map illustrates how the two configurations of track overlapped in the early years of the 20th century, though by 1912 the original lines were disused.

The pivotal event dividing the two layouts was the Poulton rail disaster of 1 July 1893. This was the first serious accident in more than 50 years of railway operation in the Fylde, but it was to accelerate much-needed improvements on the line from Preston to Blackpool and Fleetwood. Three people died and 36 were injured when a train from Talbot Road to Wigan came off the tracks as it rounded the sharp curve near the old Poulton Station at about 11 pm. The dead included the driver, Cornelius Ridgway, and a 14-year-old chorister on a church choir picnic.

The tragedy confirmed the worst fears of Poulton residents, who had long warned the railway authorities of the potential dangers of the curve, seen on the map branching at almost 90 degrees from the main line to Thornton. Even before the accident, the railway companies had been considering replacing the station.

The redevelopment was to switch the focal point of Poulton's railway system from its marginal position skirting the town at the end of Breck Road, to a hub that was nearer the town centre, where it was more accessible and had a more dominant position in the townscape.

After the deviation scheme, including about 2½ miles of new track, was opened in 1896, superfluous portions of the original main line and Blackpool branch were abandoned (though, as the 1912 map shows, the track was not immediately lifted). On 1 July 1899 a direct west-to-north Blackpool-Fleetwood curve was opened, partly following the alignment of the original Poulton-Blackpool branch, which resulted in a triangular configuration. The contractor was Thomas Wrigley.

Almost a decade later, on 12 October 1908, a wooden halt was located on the curve. This meant that Poulton, briefly, had three stations – the halt, the main station and the goods terminal at the old station. An L&Y railmotor operated the Blackpool-Fleetwood service, with 19 trains daily in each direction, and the journey time was halved to about 15 minutes. The 0-4-0 steam railmotor could seat 56 and had retractable steps for use at rail-level halts. The neat Poulton Curve Halt lasted until 1 December 1952, but the Blackpool-Fleetwood curve survived as late as November 1964, by which time the service had long since been duplicated by the seafront trams. Now the only evidence of the curve's existence is a cutting concealing the overgrown trackbed. Passenger services on the other side of the triangle, between Poulton and Fleetwood, lasted another six years, until 1970.

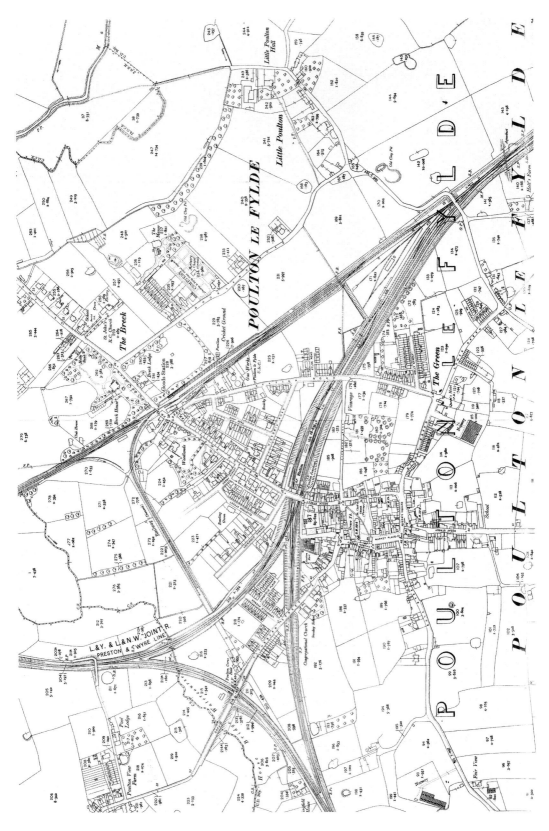

Triangles within triangles: a 1912 Ordnance Survey map of Poulton-le-Fylde. *Crown Copyright*

Right The old Poulton Station *circa* 1890. Note the part-wooden platform building, the solid signal box and (foreground, extreme left) the milk churn awaiting collection. In the background, behind the curious passengers, is Breck Road level crossing, and beyond that the line cutting across open fields towards Thornton. *Evening Gazette*

Below The replacement Poulton Station reputedly has one of the longest platforms in the provinces, and with its hanging baskets and distinctive awning has won several best-kept station awards. A new passenger lift was opened in October 1995 after a campaign by local MP Keith Mans, councillors, disability groups and Mrs Phyllis Hardman, Deputy Chairman of the North West Rail Users' Consultative Committee. The much-respected Mrs Hardman, of Knott End, who had also served as Acting Chairman, retired in 1996 after 16 years on the regional RUCC and its predecessor, the Transport Users' Consultative Committee. During that time she missed only three meetings – and those through illness – and sat on the marathon public inquiries into the closure plan for the Settle-Carlisle line. Here, workmen take advantage of a lull in traffic to attend to the track by the Blackpool-bound platform in November 1980. Poulton No 3 signal box can be glimpsed through the bridge arch. *Evening Gazette*

Above This was the scene in LMS days, with the goods yard – with its 'Admission of goods' notice – at the sharp junction of Breck Road (foreground) and Station Road; the level crossing was off the picture to the left, and the building was eventually demolished in about 1968. The Royal Oak became a makeshift casualty hospital immediately after the 1893 accident. *J. M. Tomlinson*

Below The halt at Poulton Curve was a rudimentary affair, served by the frequent trains between Blackpool North and Fleetwood. Well-maintained L&Y steam railmotor No 15 stops briefly at the ground-level 'platform', which was served by retractable steps on the train, in the early 1900s. *J. A. Peden collection*

Shortly before the First World War, an aristocratic Aspinall 'Atlantic' 4-4-2 crosses the junctions at Poulton with a Manchester express. The driver and firemen have time to pose for the photographer from the footplate of the loco, which obscures all but the roof of the signal box. The tall chimneys on the 'Atlantics' were later reduced at the L&Y's Horwich works. *John Ryan collection*

Pictured from an almost identical angle some 80 years later, this unusual shot shows a Class 47 diesel hauling an enthusiasts' special off the freight-only line from Burn Naze on to the main Blackpool-Preston route past Poulton No 3 signal box. The town boasted five signal boxes until 1971, of which No 3 – dating back to 1896 – is the sole survivor. The run-down of the ICI Hillhouse plant at Burn Naze raised a question mark about the future of the line, which had carried a thrice-weekly vinyl chloride monomer train to Barry Docks in South Wales; campaigners were hoping Railtrack would not lift the track as a result. *Paul Nettleton*

Inside Poulton No 3 are these ancient and not so ancient – but still painstakingly maintained – block signalling instruments. The wooden-cased instrument on the left could be the original, which would make it a century old and still functioning effectively. Railtrack is eventually planning to replace the Fylde's mainly semaphore system with modern colour lights. The cabin normally contains the symbolic single-line 'staff' – labelled 'Wyre Power Station' – which gives authority for a train to use the branch to ICI. There, Burn Naze South remained as a full signal box until 1987, when the level crossings on the line became crew-operated. *Paul Nettleton*

5.
THE GARSTANG &
KNOTT END RAILWAY

Cockerham Cross and Cogie Hill … Pilling and Preesall. The names roll off the tongue like a Betjemanesque evocation of a long-passed era of rural railway stations – and, in the case of a romantic but ill-starred local line, this is just what they were.

The engaging Garstang & Knott End Railway, one of the tiniest and most idiosyncratic enclaves of Britain's network, was opened on 5 December 1870. The line – nicknamed the 'Pilling Pig' because of the distinctively shrill squeal of its little locos' whistles – had harboured hopes of becoming the western tip of a grand trans-Pennine trunk route from Yorkshire and the Humberside ports.

The Garstang & Knot End (as it was initially spelled) was incorporated in 1864 to build 11½ miles of track from Garstang & Catterall Station to Knott End, which lay across the Wyre estuary from Fleetwood. It was at first something of a misnomer, extending initially only from Garstang to Pilling, and it was dogged by financial problems from the start. Between March 1872 and May 1875 services were withdrawn, but trains resumed after an official receiver was appointed.

The company continued its erratic existence until a second firm, the Knott End Railway Company, was formed to build the missing 4½-mile stretch. The plan was, typically, soon in

difficulty, but was saved by the United Alkali Company's salt operation in Preesall. The extension opened on 30 July 1908, and four years later a 1½-mile branch line was constructed to serve the salt works. As well as the principal intermediate stations at Preesall, Pilling and Garstang Town, there were halts at Cockerham Cross, Cogie Hill and Winmarleigh (renamed Nateby on 1 January 1902), and latterly Carr Lane and Garstang Road.

By 1920 the branch was carrying 53,000 tons of salt and 24,000 tons of fuel a year, and the line made a modest profit, but soon road transport was to pose a new threat. The Grouping of 1923 saw the line's five-strong loco fleet become the smallest constituent of the LMS.

On the last day of March 1930, the Knott End to Garstang passenger service was ended, and by 1947 only one goods train a day was running on the line. In 1950 the Knott End to Pilling section was shut down, and the line was finally closed 13 years later. But its impact on the Over Wyre landscape, including the early workings around Preesall, is still discernible; Fordstone Bridge, for instance, remains on the main road between Preesall and Knott End. Plans were announced in autumn 1995 to renovate the bridge after the brickwork began to crumble and an iron parapet started to rust.

Above One of the few surviving photographs of the 1876 loco *Farmer's Friend* – a name derived from the largely agricultural area served by the line. The 0-6-0 saddle tank, whose cab was later covered, is pictured with one of the original 1870 coaches. *Evening Gazette*

Below Jubilee Queen was an 0-6-0ST rather than a 4-6-0 express engine like its LMS near-namesake. The loco is pictured at Knott End soon after its introduction in 1897.

THE GARSTANG & KNOTT END RAILWAY

Left The largest loco on the line was 2-6-0T *Blackpool*, introduced in 1909, seen here behind 0-6-0ST *New Century* – from, appropriately, 1900. Unlike its tender-hauling equivalent, the 2-6-0 tank engine was one of the rarest types of British locomotive. *Blackpool*, believed to be the country's only purpose-built 2-6-0T, was ordered from builders Manning, Wardle and Co of Leeds in November 1908, six months after the smaller 0-6-0T *Knott End* had been delivered. The larger loco, dispatched the following April, used valve gear designed by the colourful but brilliant inventor Rupert John Isaacson. In 1921 *Blackpool* returned to the builders for substantial repairs, with the Isaacson valve gear being replaced by Stephenson motion. The original green livery became plain black and in 1924 the engine was renumbered LMS 11680. The loco, scrapped in 1927, is pictured after the modification to the front end of its tanks, which almost gave it the appearance of a pannier tank engine. *F. W. Shuttleworth collection*

Below left The line was also served until 1930 by an LMS (ex-LNWR) steam railmotor, No 10698, seen here from the rear at Knott End Station.

Above Garstang goods: G&KER wagon No 1, at the Birmingham Railway Carriage & Wagon Company works before delivery.

Below This American-style open-end balcony coach, No 19063, introduced in 1908, ended up on the former Caledonian Railway's Wanlockhead branch in the Scottish Highlands – the highest point on the LMS network. The end of an ex-Garstang van can also be seen on the right. *All F. W. Shuttleworth collection*

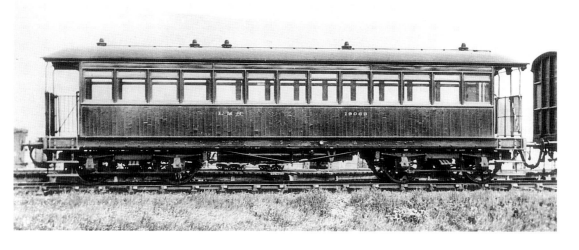

THE GARSTANG & KNOTT END RAILWAY

Four contrasting views of Garstang Town Station. The first (*above*), from the end of the 19th century, shows the simple track layout at the station. The second (*below*) was taken in 1909 – a year after the Pilling to Knott End extension opened. The loading gauge and goods shed are visible in both pictures, but the later shot shows the more extensive yard following the increase in business on the line.

However, the third picture (*above right*) shows a vista of

RAILWAYS OF BLACKPOOL AND THE FYLDE

dereliction in April 1964, with broken windows, weed-encrusted platforms, peeling paintwork and abandoned sleepers littering the scene. The station building and goods shed have been reduced to dilapidated hulks, and the loading gauge, footbridge and signal have gone, though a water column remains. The picture is taken from the opposite end of the station from the previous one; the carriage sheds can be seen in the distance. The fourth photograph (*below*) provides a closer view of the crumbling carriage sheds on the same day.

After the closure of the Knott End to Pilling section in 1950, Garstang remained open for the daily Preston freight until 1 August 1963, when it became a coal depot before final closure on 16 August 1965. After demolition, the only clue to its existence was a housing estate approached from Station Way. *John Ryan collection (2)/ F. W. Shuttleworth (2)*

Above Little sign of life as a lone cyclist prepares to negotiate the level crossing at Pilling Station in 1928. Today a brightly painted, flower-bedecked railway handcart near the site of the former station bears testimony to the fact that the village once enjoyed a quintessential rural rail link. *John Ryan collection*

Below Yorkshire artillerymen and their officers arrive at an uncharacteristically busy Knott End in 1909 for exercises. Behind the military wagons to the left is the clerestory of a passenger coach, while the goods yard on the right is bustling with equipment. *John Ryan collection*

Above Contrast the packed platform in the 1909 picture with the handful of passengers at the resolutely rural Knott End terminus in about 1911. *Knott End* has arrived with a three-coach train from Garstang. Note the water tower in the distance. *J. A. Peden collection*

Below A picture taken from almost the same angle 40 years later, in June 1951. Seven months earlier the Knott End terminus had been closed, and weeds are already beginning to reclaim the platforms and track. Structures visible (from left) are the stationmaster's house, the water tower, the signal box and the goods shed. *C. A. Appleton*

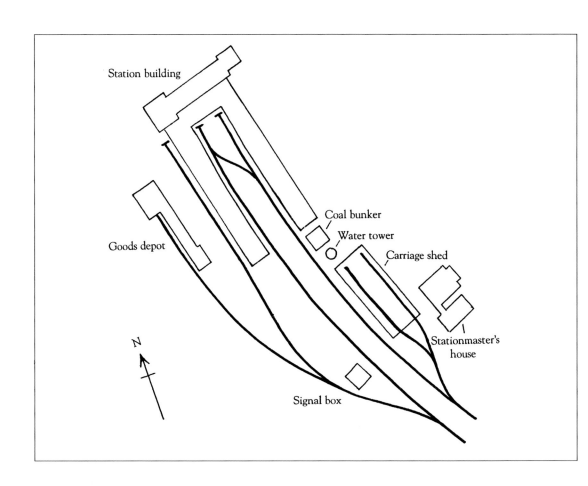

Station building

Coal bunker

Water tower

Goods depot

Carriage shed

Stationmaster's house

N

Signal box

Above left A sketch plan showing the locations of the principal features of the station.

Below left, above and below Three views of Knott End Station on 5 April 1964, 14 years after its closure: the station building viewed towards the buffers; the platforms cut to allow access to a car park under construction; and the former goods shed looking towards Garstang. *All F. W. Shuttleworth*

Well-wishers swarm over Ivatt '2MT' 2-6-0 No 46429 – and the driver receives a consolatory cuppa – as it prepares to pull the final train from Knott End Station on 13 November 1950. Bill Wilkinson, who is now one of Lancashire's leading freelance newspaper and magazine photographers, recalls, 'The closure of the Pilling Pig was the first assignment I covered when I became a press photographer.'

Today it is commemorated by a colourful model of the train featuring an eye-catching floral display. 'It was nice to see the old train had been remembered in this way,' says Bill. *Evening Gazette*

6.
OFF THE BEATEN TRACKS

The Fylde has had its fair share of small railway systems, Lilliputian steam locos and diminutive diesels operating on industrial, preserved and miniature lines.

Salwick and Lea Road, on the Blackpool-Preston route, were the only two stations on the heavily-used stretch of track east of Kirkham and were completed to an almost identical design. Lea Road opened in 1842 and Salwick soon after, both subsequently situated between the slow lines. Long-vanished Lea Road closed on 2 May 1938, as did Salwick, but the latter re-opened on a restricted basis on 8 April 1940 and to regular passenger traffic on 2 November 1942. Salwick signal box, a fringe cabin to Preston power box, also survives (but not the two fast lines). Unlike the Blackpool North to Kirkham section, on the majority of which traditional block semaphore signalling operates, the Salwick section to Preston is controlled by colour light signals.

On the overgrown western edge of the station stood the remains of a decorative wishing-well, built in stone but long since emptied of water. Nearby, in steam days, thirsty engines welcomed the water troughs on the former quadruple stretch of track between Preston and Kirkham. The island platform once boasted attractive flower beds and lamps, and a canopy supported on cast iron columns outside brick buildings. Today there is just a bus-shelter type structure, though part of the platform has a tiled mosaic floor, and trains stop there a handful of times a day.

The reason for the station's unlikely existence lies immediately to the east – the British Nuclear Fuels' Springfields plant. A direct connection linked the main line with the BNFL plant's own internal railway operation behind the factory's high fences. The plant, which started production after the war, was served by extensive sidings.

Today the former Lea Road Station has been obliterated from the landscape. However, this August 1966 picture, looking towards Preston, shows its weed-covered island platform still in place between the slow lines, almost 30 years after its closure. Unlike its sister at Salwick, the road passes beneath rather than above the station. *Jack Fenton*

Railway guard Ray Ruffell leans from the cab of one of the BNFL Hudswells in 1983 as he sought to travel on every stretch of track in the country. *Evening Gazette*

For almost half a century, two 35-ton 0-4-0 diesel shunters, bought from their Leeds-based manufacturer during the Second World War, hauled chemical tankers and freight wagons loaded with equipment around the internal railway network. When BNFL bosses announced that they were making the pair of Hudswell Clarke locos redundant, a group of workers stepped in to launch an on-site preservation group.

A dozen employees, headed by site visits officer Eric Bond, set up SHAME – Springfields Hudswell-Clarke Appreciation and Maintenance Enterprise. No 628 – nicknamed, inevitably, the 'Mighty Atom' – was restored to its original bright red and green bodywork in time for the 50th anniversary of its shipment to Salwick on 10 December 1993. BNFL top brass were on hand to inspect its gleaming brasses in an anniversary ceremony at the site. Also present was one of the original drivers of the loco, Bill Hudson, aged 84. The unveiling ceremony was performed by Pamela Murphy, a pupil of Lea Endowed CE Primary School.

Its sister, No 629, was to have left for the Bury-based preserved East Lancashire Railway to be restored in a BNFL blue livery. SHAME also raised money to buy a Gloucester DMU driving trailer to convert into an education train – a travelling classroom for visiting schoolchildren. In 1995, however, BNFL announced that it was developing the site of the former engine shed, and much of the internal track network was lifted. Almost half a mile was given to the Embsay Steam Railway, and the two locos were transferred to Southport Railway Centre, which was due to relocate to an ambitious new heritage complex at the former Preston Docks for the Millennium.

As for the passenger service from Salwick Station, residents signed a petition in 1993 for a more extensive timetable. They sent the signatures to Fylde MP Michael Jack, who has championed rail services to some of the more remote areas of his constituency.

Below left and right The Fylde's other big industrial railway was at ICI's Hillhouse plant at Burn Naze near Thornton. The line was used to transport chemical raw materials to the complex and finished products from it. The works, now much contracted, employed 3,500 in its heyday in the 1970s. As the plant was run down, only occasionally did tanker trains, carrying chemicals or oil, negotiate the points at Poulton to branch off down the single line bound for ICI. Development of the Hillhouse internal railway, which encircled the site, was stimulated by industrial activity on the opposite side of the Wyre. In 1872 a Barrow-in-Furness haematite company discovered rich salt deposits while searching for iron ore in Preesall. By 1893 rock salt was being carried to Preesall jetty, and brine was being piped across the estuary to Fleetwood Salt Works. In 1890 the salt works was taken over by the United Alkali Company, and by 1926 it had become part of the worldwide operations of Imperial Chemical Industries. In the first picture demolition begins on the minehead buildings from which rock salt was carried by rail to the jetty at Preesall, while the second shows an enclosed ICI salt wagon, with a capacity of 10 tons, in Burn Naze sidings as a shunting loco gets up steam in the background on the left, at the foot of one of the chimneys. *Evening Gazette/ICI*

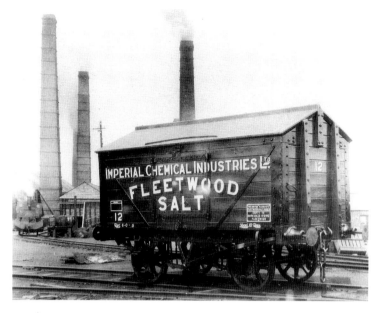

Below Like Salwick, Hillhouse was served by a passenger station, Burn Naze. At least 500 trains passed under Burn Naze bridge to and from Fleetwood every week as late as the 1950s. Here a vintage Aspinall-designed, Horwich-built ex-L&Y heavy goods 0-8-0 steams through Burn Naze with a freight train from Fleetwood on 9 June 1951, almost half a century after the loco's introduction. *C. A. Appleton*

Above In 1918 the L&Y and LNWR sought powers to build a branch from the station at Thornton to Cleveleys, but instead reached an agreement under which the Blackpool and Fleetwood tramway was linked to the railway at the port's Copse Road tram depot. A 10-ton steeple cab electric tram engine hauled trains of mineral wagons from the connecting line behind the depot to the coal sidings at Thornton Gate, Cleveleys. The engine, pictured at the National Tramway Museum at Crich in Derbyshire, had been bought in 1923 from the English Electric Company. It operated from 1925, when the sidings were constructed, until 30 April 1949, when coal supplies were diverted to Layton and Thornton.

Young Stan Croasdale had one of the most unusual jobs in the transport industry – a shunter's mate on a tramway system. His first permanent post with Blackpool Corporation involved him standing in front of the empty wagons taken to Copse Road with red and green flags. This was the only means of signalling to the driver that the road in front was clear of tramcars. The empty wagons were left on a spare line running up the side of the tramshed connecting to the railway tracks, and the full wagons, each weighing about 18 tons loaded, would be coupled up. Stan retired in 1986 after becoming the most senior tram driver on the staff, having completed 44 years with the corporation.

Below In 1992 Fleetwood Locomotive Centre sought to run its four renovated steam engines and three diesels from Poulton to the Broadwater Caravan Park, which would

have involved adding half a mile of track near Fleetwood Dock. The Locomotive Centre, formerly based on spare land at ICI Hillhouse, was formed in 1981 under the chairmanship of ebullient steam buff Chris Moore. It acquired a wide-ranging roster of renowned locos, from ex-Great Western 'Hall' Class 4-6-0 No 4979 *Wootton Hall* to Stanier 'Black Five' 4-6-0 No 45491. The centre was later based on the former Fleetwood Power Station site, but its collection was subsequently to become a feature of the new Preston complex.

Need a good set of wheels, mister? The photograph shows Chris Moore in the mid-1980s working on the disembodied driving wheels of No 45491 at the group's former base at ICI Thornton. *Evening Gazette*

Top The Locomotive Centre's Poulton link plan was revived in 1994 by businessman Michael Taylor with backing from MPs, Wyre Council and the Rail Link '84 group. Mr Taylor, Chairman of Hambleton-based Carr Royd Leisure, envisaged running tourism-based steam services between Fleetwood and a new terminus close to the main line at Poulton, linked by a walkway to the existing station. Here *Wootton Hall* suffers the temporary indignity – although for its ultimate benefit – of being carried piggy-back-style by a low-loader lorry from Barry scrapyard for restoration at the Loco Centre in 1986. *Evening Gazette*

Middle At the other end of the coast, contraction was the order of the day. The branch to the small but bustling dock at Lytham had been one of the original features of the South Fylde line when it opened in 1846. From June 1865 to May 1874 it was served by Warton (Lytham Dock) Station, and there was later a short-lived Warton Halt, which was closed by 1923. In 1969, however, a unique collection of railwayana opened to the public in Dock Road, Lytham. The Lytham Motive Power Museum housed five historic locos, including a rare 1887 North British Railway 0-4-0 saddle tank, No 68095. The museum was founded by rail enthusiast Jim Morris, Managing Director of the adjacent company, Helical Springs, who is pictured (centre) with fellow directors Derek Hudson (left) and Arthur Allen and a trio of saddle tanks in 1967 before the museum's public opening. *Evening Gazette*

Bottom When the recession took its toll on the parent company, Mr Morris reluctantly had to sell his collection in March 1992. The NBR tank went, fittingly, to the Scottish Railway Preservation Society. This line drawing shows another of the rarities at the now-disbanded Lytham Creek Museum, *Johnathon*, a Hunslet 0-4-0ST built in 1898.

In the next-door resort of St Annes, however, the preserved rail traffic was inward rather than outward as a static steam train was moved to the Pleasure Island complex in 1993. The train, with former BR carriages housing shops, bar and restaurant, was installed by the owner of the complex, Carr Royd Leisure. It is 'hauled' by 0-4-0 saddle tank *Daphne*.

The Fylde's most comprehensive range of railwayana is owned by acclaimed local collector and rail expert Jim Kay, who has spent years amassing a superb array of memorabilia from the coast's lines and elsewhere. His collection includes everything from a complete set of station nameboards from the Blackpool Central line to station doors, benches, crockery, signals and levers, mileposts, track plans, share certificates, tickets, timetables and a magnificent clock from the original Preston & Wyre Railway. His collection is not only a treasure trove for rail-

lovers but also an invaluable source of historical information about the coast's railway network over the past 150 years.

Blackpool Pleasure Beach has its own elaborate miniature railway, with authentic-outline locos working on 21-inch gauge track. One of the highlights of the journey was this scale replica of the Forth Bridge (since removed) crossing the edge of the boating lake. The bridge is seen here in two pre-war views, one in daytime and the other brightly illuminated beneath the Big Dipper. The line was the successor to the world's first 15-inch gauge miniature railway, which had been built on the site by W. J. Bassett-Lowke in 1905. Bassett-Lowke's 4-4-2 engine was described by the *Railway Magazine* as 'the most perfect model locomotive' to be constructed in this country. Unfortunately, blown sand clogging the axle-boxes put paid to the original railway after four years' operation. *Commercial postcards*

Right The Pleasure Beach Express fleet of one-third-scale diesel-powered locos includes the 'Pacifics' *Princess Royal* (pictured) and *Mary Louise* and the 4-6-4T *Carol Jean*, the last two named after the children of chairman Mrs Doris Thompson, daughter of Alderman Bean, and her late husband Leonard. The line boasts a palatial terminus modelled on 1920s LMS stations in the Fylde, complete with elaborately decorated steelwork, impressive awning, booking office, signal box, water tower and, unusually for a miniature railway, a set of working freight stock.

The original *Carol Jean* was destroyed in a devastating fire on 18 July 1934, but this provided Leonard Thompson, then Managing Director, with the spur to rebuild the line on an even grander scale. From the Golden Acre Park Miniature Railway in Leeds, the family acquired a set of rolling-stock built by Hudswell Clarke, including an enclosed 1st Class dining car, in maroon livery, which still plies the line today at the rear. Since 1934 the line, an irregular continuous loop, has meandered through the southern end of the Pleasure Beach for almost a mile in the shadow of its famous white-knuckle rides. It shares part of the route with the pioneering 1966 monorail and cleverly curls beneath the latest and most dramatic addition to the skyscape, the Pepsi Max Big One – the world's tallest and fastest roller-coaster.

Below A Class 142 'Pacer' unit breaks a banner to mark the opening of the BR station at the Pleasure Beach on 13 April 1987. The station sowed the seeds of confusion for some passengers – such as the man who asked the driver of the

amusement park's miniature railway, Teddy Askey, to take him to Salford! Teddy, who has spent more than three decades on the fun-park footplate, is one of the best-loved characters on the Pleasure Beach and in August 1995 was featured on a national network radio programme. The following year he was awarded the MBE for his services to tourism, but chose to receive his medal at County Hall, Preston, rather than Buckingham Palace. 'I'm born and bred in Lancashire and that's where I want to enjoy this award,' he explained.

The new station was financed jointly by the amusement park, BR, Lancashire County Council and Blackpool Council. Since the late 1980s the Pleasure Beach and the railway have been seeking to renew the marriage of mutual benefit that existed with the LMS. They launched a highly successful joint promotion, which over three years saw more than £1.1 million of ride tickets sold to rail passengers. *Evening Gazette*

BLACKPOOL PLEASURE BEACH STATION

Left Half a dozen miniature railways have operated at Fylde Coast locations, including Fleetwood, Cleveleys, St Annes and Blackpool Zoo in East Park Drive. At historic Marsh Mill in Thornton, the Fylde Society of Model Engineers shares its fine collection of more than 30 miniature locos with the public on its 1,050-foot-long track. The group was formed in the 1920s and has about 60 members, from school age to enthusiasts in their 80s.

On a smaller scale, OO-gauge model railways operated in part of the former station buildings at Blackpool South and, briefly, the Pleasure Beach. But more sophisticated public tastes heralded the demise of some of the Fylde's tiny trains. Fleetwood, however, lost its miniature railway as the result of a more insidious problem – vandalism. The port-cum-resort had acquired a miniature railway in 1954, operating smaller-scale versions of famous British locos, including ex-Southern Railway Bulleid 'Pacific' No 34051 *Sir Winston Churchill*. The loco gives bystanders on the bridge a splendid display as it hauls a well-loaded 'Golden Arrow' soon after the line's launch. *Evening Gazette*

Below The original Fleetwood miniature line linked the Marine Hall Gardens with the boating lake. A second, mile-long railway was opened in 1975, closer to the sea than the original, with a run-round loop at each end. By now the American influence was being felt in the shape of a Western-style Severn Lamb Rio Grande 2-8-0 steam-outline loco, bought from the 15-inch gauge Blackpool Zoo railway, which had opened in 1972. Despite its attractive location, however, the Fleetwood line was closed in 1983 and its toast-rack carriages and track were sold to the Port Erroll Railway in Scotland. *Evening Gazette*

Above Steam on the seafront: this was Blackpool's Sands Express, an improvised line along which steam locos hauled columns of trucks during a promenade-widening project in 1911. Here 1903 0-6-0 saddle tank *Reliance* thunders along the prom with a wagon-load of sand near North Pier. The Express was the creation of James Brodie, the redoubtable Borough Engineer of Blackpool, who masterminded the scheme to build a 500-yard concrete wall between North Pier and Cocker Street and fill the gap with 226,000 tons of sand. The line had no ballast: the sleepers were laid directly on the asphalt surface. Note the elaborate protection on the loco against wind-blown sand. *Evening Gazette*

Below Another of the 0-6-0 saddle tanks that made up the five-strong Sands Express fleet steams spectacularly past the Tower and Palace entertainments complex. Four of the locos were built by Manning Wardle: *Annie*, *Netherton*, *Horbury* and *Reliance*. The fifth, *Alice*, was a Hudswell Clarke engine. *Evening Gazette*

CONSTRUCTING NEW CENTRAL PROMENADE, BLACKPOOL

Above Almost a decade before the Sands Express, an earlier promenade-widening project saw the creation of a colossal extension of the seafront at Central Beach. A revolutionary feature was the segregated tram track, seen here being laid while a Dreadnought car passes on the existing street tracks. In the background of this scene of coastal chaos can be seen the wooden 'jetty' along which sand from the beach was pumped to fill the cavity between the old promenade

RAILWAYS OF BLACKPOOL AND THE FYLDE

and the new sea wall at an estimated rate of 165 tons an hour. This rare postcard of the three-year widening scheme nearing completion is from 1905, the year the new Central Promenade opened.

The famous Blackpool tramway can hardly be categorised alongside miniature railways – it is a highly efficient people-mover operating on 4 ft 8½ in track. Opened in 1885 and originally using the conduit system, the world's first electric street tramway was complemented 13 years later by the cliff-top Blackpool & Fleetwood Tramroad. The two systems were joined at Gynn Square in 1919. The Blackpool network was extended along a series of suburban routes, including Marton, Layton and Squires Gate, as well as New South Promenade. *Commercial postcard*

Below left The Sands Express wasn't the last time 'steam' ran on the prom. Introducing the most unusual locomotive in Blackpool – this illuminated mock-up of an American Sante Fe engine and carriage was built in 1962 from two former tramcars. With its cow-catcher and bell, the colourful Western-style tram takes trippers on specials during the Illuminations, with the driver sitting in the glass-fronted 'smokebox'. The 'train', which is pictured with a 'balloon' and an open 'boat' tram, retains its trolley pole, but most members of the fleet now boast pantographs.

In May 1963 the 'train' took VIP guests to the opening of the new ABC Theatre in Church Street, featuring a show starring Cliff Richard and the Shadows. The trip raised some eyebrows as the length of track had officially closed the year before. Indeed, the early 1960s saw the closure of the entire inland network, with only the seafront section remaining. Even so, there have been proposals for a light rail system linking both BR and tramway tracks from Fleetwood to Kirkham.

Above The Fylde's latest item of miniaturised transport is a tiny tram: the Blackpool North Pier Tramway. This marked the completion of one of the first entirely new pier railways in Britain for more than 80 years. Pier owner First Leisure Corporation awarded the contract for the work to Harry Steer Engineering of Derbyshire as part of a major refurbishment of the Victorian structure. The vehicle, containing three carriages with a total capacity of 56, operates on a 250-metre, 3-foot-gauge track on the strengthened north edge of the pier. Here one of the carriages is lifted delicately into place by crane from the beach in readiness for the line's opening on 2 September 1991. The pier is now owned by Leisure Parcs, which bought most of the First Leisure attractions – including the Tower and Winter Gardens – in 1998.

7.
MEN AND MACHINES

The Steam Era

The Fylde Coast was a final enclave of steam in 1968 – the year Alexander Dubcek's Prague Spring was crushed and Robert Kennedy and Martin Luther King were assassinated. It would be foolhardy, of course, to compare the demise of standard gauge steam power on British Railways to these earth-shattering global events, but the eclipse of steam did have a potent impact on many Britons' lives and emotions. As steam operation contracted to a small outpost in Lancashire, the exhaust plumes from work-weary engines still rose over the Fylde fields. After August 1968, however, the distinctive sight, sound and smell of steam were replaced by the utilitarian drone of diesel.

The first locomotives used in the Fylde, during the period of mid-Victorian expansion, had largely been workhorse single-wheelers: they ruled the railway roost on the peninsula until the final quarter of the 19th century. As locomotive technology proceeded apace, however, they were superseded by a new generation of express locomotives, most notably in the Fylde by the powerful 'Atlantic' 4-4-2s. The engines were developed in the workshops and design offices of the Lancashire & Yorkshire Railway, which ran the Fylde lines in a two-thirds/one-third partnership with the London & North Western. The L&Y Chief Mechanical Engineer, Sir John Aspinall, introduced the unique inside cylinder 4-4-2 locos in 1899 and they, with the four cylinder 4-6-0s that came out nine years later, had charge of the main Blackpool-Manchester workings until well into LMS days.

The huge 7 ft 3 in driving wheels of the 'Atlantics' earned them the sobriquet 'High Flyers'. Their sheer size was awe-inspiring and they had the biggest boiler so far seen in Britain. Until then the premier engines on the system had been Aspinall's 'Flyer' 4-4-0s working from major sheds like Blackpool and Newton Heath.

A thirsty Aspinall 4-4-0 takes water at the head of an L&Y Blackpool express early in the 20th century. *Commercial postcard*

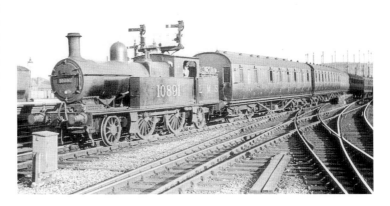

Incidentally, the running shed foreman for the L&Y at Blackpool Central at the turn of the century was young H. N. (later Sir Nigel) Gresley, who married the daughter of a Lytham solicitor.

In 1908 George Hughes, as the L&Y's CME (Aspinall was by then General Manager), carried out superheating trials on four 4-4-0s, which transformed both their appearance and performance. The following year they were fitted with Walschaerts valve gear and new boilers with a Schmidt superheater and extended smokebox. Two – numbers 1098 and 1110 – were shedded at Blackpool. The improved performance was immediately apparent and compared favourably with that of the 'Atlantics'.

Also in 1908 Hughes unveiled the final class of L&Y express passenger locos. The imposing 4-6-0, with its 6 ft 3 in coupled wheels, was named *Dreadnought* after the impenetrable battleship. But, initially at least, its performance did not match its formidable appearance. The 20 engines produced in 1908 and 1909 were despatched to a series of sheds, including Blackpool. However, the 'Dreadnought' fleet had to be substantially rebuilt from 1920 after suffering a spate of mechanical problems. Although scrapping of the 'Dreadnoughts' had begun as early as 1925, there were still ten of the Hughes 4-6-0s stabled at Blackpool on the outbreak of the Second World War, painted in the immaculate crimson livery reserved for the principal passenger locos. Six lasted into the British Railways era and the last – No 50455 – ended its days at

Blackpool shed before being broken up in October 1951. Three months earlier, the loco had hauled an 11-carriage excursion from Central to York on a balmy day in July. It was the last L & Y express engine in service.

The Fylde passenger scene was dominated by the steam aristocracy, but during the peak holiday season anything that could raise steam was pressed into service. Indeed, one of the phenomena of the Fylde was the sheer diversity of the locos that could be seen there during the holiday season. There were, of course, Stanier 'Black Five' 4-6-0s and Hughes-Fowler 'Crab' 2-6-0s. There were also 'Jubilees' – often named evocatively after the dominions of the British Empire – powerful 'Patriots' and sometimes ex-LNER 'B1' 4-6-0s. There were 'Britannia' 4-6-2s, Class '9F' 2-10-0s and Stanier '8F' 2-8-0s. There were LMS '4P' 2-6-4 and '3F' 0-6-0 tanks alongside gleaming 'Royal Scots', which were mainly used on scheduled services, as were some 'Jubilees' and 'Patriots'. There was even a memorable summer visit by 'A4' 'Pacific' 4-6-2 No 60022 *Mallard*. Yet the old rivalries of the pre-Grouping era still survived. Former Blackpool footplateman Fred Laycock, a member of the Blackpool & Fylde Rail Users' Association, remembered ex-LNWR engines from Preston still being entered on the board as 'foreigners' in the solidly L&Y Blackpool shed.

Even as late as the summer of 1964, the enthusiast could see a collection of motive power unparalleled outside the major cities. When Central shed closed on 30 July 1964, the resident 'Jubilee', No 45574 *India*, was

MANCHESTER & BLACKPOOL EXPRESS.

LONDON MIDLAND & SCOTTISH RLY.
LANCASHIRE & YORKSHIRE SECTION.

A gleaming 'Dreadnought' 4-6-0, in early LMS days though still with its lined L&Y livery and company name on the tender, splashes through the troughs on a Manchester to Blackpool express in the 1920s. *Commercial postcard*

specially cleaned and painted for the 10.15 am service to Manchester Victoria.

The big problem at Blackpool was the lack of an automated coaling plant. Former Blackpool driver and fireman Don Rutter recalled toiling by hand to fill tenders at Central – which, with a loco consuming some 8 tons of coal on a run to London, was a Herculean job. The old coaling stage could not keep up with demand on the busiest days, which meant some engines having to be refuelled at Preston or Lostock Hall.

The end of steam had been decreed in the BR modernisation plan of 1955, but the effect of the new policy was barely noticeable until the early 1960s, when the pace of withdrawals was accelerated. Even so, the travelling public remained understandably more concerned about the cuts in the size of the network proposed in the Beeching report in 1963. By January 1968 there were just 13 steam depots left in the country, most of them in the North West – including Rose Grove (near Burnley), Lostock Hall (Preston) and Carnforth (near Lancaster). As the end of steam grew still closer, this trio of towns shared the sad distinction of

being the final bastions of working steam engines at their motive power depots.

The decline of steam was symbolised most poignantly by the scene in Blackpool North shed on 15 May 1968. 'Black Five' No 45444 stood forlornly in the depot, stripped of its smokebox numberplate. However, its identity had been defiantly re-established by an enthusiast who had painstakingly hand-painted the numbers in white-on-red characters.

Steam traction, however, enjoyed something of an Indian Summer on the Fylde Coast. Right to the end, on 4 August 1968 – the final day of standard gauge steam traction in scheduled service on BR – Rose Grove was still turning out engines to take coal from the Lancashire pits to Wyre Dock for Fleetwood power station.

On 4 August enthusiasts' societies chartered steam-hauled trains from six towns to mark the final day. The following weekend, the famous 'Fifteen Guinea Special' saw the 'Britannia' 'Pacific' *Oliver Cromwell* – helped by three 'Black Fives' – take charge of a sentimental Last Day of Steam excursion from Liverpool and Manchester to Carlisle. But preservationists were to ensure that steam would survive.

RAILWAYS OF BLACKPOOL AND THE FYLDE

Top LMS 'Patriot' No 5524 *Blackpool* handled the crack Blackpool and Fylde Coast Express, which clocked up some impressive timings between the resort and London Euston. Blackpool's eponymous 'Patriot' was named in a ceremony in March 1937 by the Mayor, Alderman Ashton, who smashed a bottle of champagne against its boiler in time-honoured fashion. Escaping rebuilding after the war, the 1933-built loco remained in its original condition until withdrawn as BR No 45524 in 1962. *Evening Gazette*

Middle Blackpool wasn't the only Fylde coast town to have a 'Patriot' loco named after it. No 45546 was named *Fleetwood*, and is seen here ready for duty with its old-style tender at Edge Hill depot, Liverpool, in 1961, while No 45548 carried *Lytham St Annes* nameplates. *Locofotos*

Bottom This was another engine commemorating part of North Fylde in its name. LNWR 'Precedent' Class 2-4-0 No 1166 was named *Wyre*, after the river on which Fleetwood was developed and, no doubt, the old Preston & Wyre Railway. F. W. Webb's locos, which had 6 ft 6 in driving wheels, were capable of hauling prodigious loads, though *Wyre* is seen with a relatively modest four-carriage train in the early 1900s.

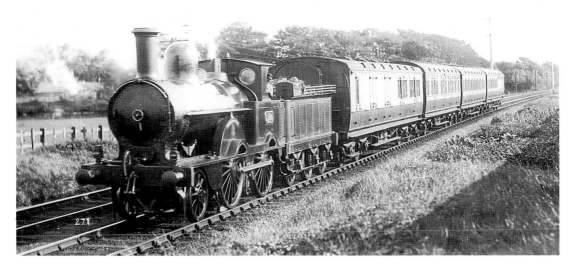

Above The quintessence of Fylde Coast steam: 'Black Five' No 45068 is ready for the flag on the uncovered excursion platforms at Central Station, probably on a special to Windermere. *Don Rutter*

Below In April 1968 Fleetwood steam stalwarts turned out in force when 'Britannia' Class 4-6-2 No 70013 *Oliver Cromwell* made a valedictory visit to Wyre Dock Station. *Evening Gazette*

Don Rutter: footplate photographer

Life on the footplate of a steam locomotive wasn't as cosily romantic as many steam enthusiasts would imagine. A runaway train, a drainpipe smashing into the cab, and extremes of heat and cold … these are just some of the less than fond memories lodged in the mind of Fylde photographer and former footplateman Don Rutter. Yet driver Don, an accomplished cameraman, is among the millions who mourn the passing of steam despite having witnessed its down-side as well as its delights. An Associate of the Royal Photographic Society, he recorded the last days of steam at Blackpool Central Station to build up an atmospheric library of pictures of the much-missed terminus.

Don started work as an engine cleaner at the old Rigby Road motive power depot in 1954. Chargehand cleaner Teddy Ash, a small, bespectacled figure with only one arm, told the apprentices what they had to do. They committed the rule book to memory until, one day, they became 'passed cleaners'. They worked shifts, longing for a chance to act as firemen, even if only on the station pilot, shunting carriages into and out of Central.

Eventually Don did graduate to the footplate. After a demanding three-day examination, conducted by a footplate inspector called Bill Marsden, resplendent in a bowler hat, he became a 'passed fireman', which allowed him to undertake driving duties. He served mainly on the Manchester, Liverpool and East Lancashire lines, on the footplate of 'Black Five' and 'Jubilee' locos, before moving on to the London and Crewe services in the cab of English Electric 2,000 hp Type 4 (Class 40) diesel locomotives. Working from both Blackpool North and Central Stations, he was often teamed with affable Alf Chew, one of the most easy-going drivers on the network.

Don has been taking pictures since leaving school at 15 and has exhibited his work all over Lancashire. The evocative black-and-white shots of Central in the years immediately before its closure conjure up a poignant picture of the last days of steam, though these days his work is mainly on colour slides, using a 35 mm camera. He is competitions secretary and a past President of the Blackpool & Fylde Photographic Society and is a judge and lecturer for the Lancashire & Cheshire Photographic Society.

Don at the controls of a Manchester-bound 'Black Five'.

Above With the concentration on the mechanical and technical, it's sometimes forgotten that it was people – as well as machines – that were the mainstay of the railway. Don Rutter recorded his workmates as well as the engines they operated. Here, a group of passed cleaners/firemen stands by the massive driving wheels of 'Royal Scot' Class 4-6-0 No 46167 *The Hertfordshire Regiment* at Rigby Road MPD in 1958. They are (from left) George Kent, Peter Smith, Bill Thompson, Dave Walker and Cyril Hawley.

Left Passed fireman Ken Davis and fireman Charlie Hogarth await departure with the 2 pm Blackpool Central-Manchester train in 1960.

Above and above right Not a loco in sight as these two railmen, brothers George (left) and Bill Davis, trek along the tracks from Central; and driver Dick Fenton keeps the driving wheels well-oiled on another loco alongside the planked section of platform at Central. Dick narrowly escaped with his life when a fishplate crashed through the front window of a DMU he was driving, killing a passenger.

Right The two classic images of early 1960s transport were the motor scooter and its considerably more powerful counterpart, the grimy 'Black Five'. Here, fireman Doug Dunstan stands astride his scooter at Rigby Road. Doug, who suffered kidney failure, later moved to Crewe, where shed staff organised a region-wide collection to buy him a dialysis machine so he could have treatment at home after two transplants. This helped him stay with the railway until his retirement almost 30 years later.

This page The end of another busy shift for driver Bill Fisher (just visible in his cab) and fireman J. P. Smith (back to camera in the first picture and walking away in the second) as they turn their 'Black Five' No 44819 at Rigby Road MPD before it goes off for fire-cleaning, re-coaling, watering and shedding. One of the most important parts of this picture (at least from a railwayman's viewpoint) is in the background – the pay office! The man in the beret is fire-dropper Bill Evans.

Right Coal and diesel: English Electric Type 4 (Class 40) No D210 Empress of Britain stands alongside a small pile of coal at Crewe where it has arrived from Blackpool Central on driver training duties in the early 1960s. Instructor Ernie Bellamy (centre) shares a joke with drivers Alex Harvey (left) and Bill Davis. All three were based at Blackpool.

A smiling Les Skinn at the controls of a Blackpool 'Black Five'; believe it or not he had a friend, also a driver, called Bill Bone! Les was a highly rated footballer, although Skinn and Bone sounded more like a double-act on Central Pier than Central Station.

Men on the line

It was the day Bill Baildon finally came home ... to a windswept platform 4 at Blackpool North Station. In scenes more reminiscent of a ship launch, almost 200 people packed the platform to the skirl of bagpipes for a unique locomotive-naming ceremony in January 1993.

Former colleagues and friends of William Henry Baildon, who had died exactly a year earlier, watched as Regional Railways North West immortalised the memory of the engine driver known affectionately as 'Our Eli'. The late Councillor Dorothy Preston, who was then the Mayor of Blackpool, pulled back a curtain to reveal the gleaming nameplate *Our Eli* on the side of Class 31/4 loco No 31455 in Regional Railways blue and white livery. Blackpool-based Mr Baildon died of cancer at the age of 55 after a railway career that began at 14 in the old Blackpool Central engine shed and spanned more than four decades. His father, also a railwayman, had been known as 'Old Eli', so it was logical that Mr Baildon Jnr should be dubbed 'Our Eli'.

✳ ✳ ✳

Blackpool's railway renaissance man Michael Carr – councillor, union official, former railway guard, porter and signalman, clarinettist and Promenade concert-goer – had more than enough to keep him occupied during his enforced retirement from the railway through ill-health.

Mr Carr, Vice-Chairman of Blackpool Council's Transport Committee, had a walk-on part in some of Britain's greatest political dramas. He was on duty at Central Station on one of the most momentous days in British politics when half the Conservative Cabinet arrived for the 1963 party conference – two days before the resignation of Prime Minister Harold Macmillan. And he helped Labour firebrand Aneurin Bevan to carry his luggage on to the train after his powerful speech to the party's otherwise sombre post-election conference in 1959. The following year the MP was dead.

Mr Carr regrets the passing of the old school of railway manager, typified by former Blackpool Central and North stationmaster Bill Atkinson: 'He was the boss and he let you know it, but he was fair and honest. You would do anything for him.'

This attitude was crystallised during the Weeton disaster of 16 July 1961, when Mr Carr's day began in the quiet of a shunter's cabin at 4 am and ended 16 hours later. All the trains diverted from the Blackpool North line were channelled into Central.

Mr Atkinson retired in 1973 after 48 years on the railway – 'a man of strength,' according to his son, John, 'who had worked his way up from the bottom.' He died in 1992 at the age of 81.

Right 'Our Eli' educates: Bill Baildon (centre) provides boiler instruction on a 2,000 hp English Electric diesel loco to J. P. Smith (left) and Bobby Bryan. Until electrically heated carriages came on the scene in 1964, most diesels needed boilers to provide steam for carriage heating, and these had to be filled up from water troughs or towers. *Don Rutter*

Below The tribute to Bill Baildon was the idea of fellow driver Alan Deamer, who helped organise a collection that raised £190 for the plates and a set of commemorative mugs. Newton Replicas made the four plates – two for the loco, a third for a staff room and the fourth to be auctioned for cancer charities. Another loco of the same class – No 31411 – had already been operating unofficially with *Our Eli* plates the previous summer before Regional Railways management decided to formalise the unusual tribute. The fourth nameplate was bought at auction by record producer and railway collector Pete Waterman. Here *Our Eli* drifts through a leafy Layton Station with a Liverpool-Blackpool North service in 1994. *Paul Nettleton*

Mr Carr also has a background firmly rooted in the railway, being the son of a railwayman, Harold, and his wife Eleanor.

* * *

In 1930 Tom Barker started work as a 15-year-old 'bar boy' at the two Blackpool sheds, but was made redundant after about two years when the recession set in.

'It was all night work – two weeks at Rigby Road and one at Talbot Road,' he recalls. 'I certainly know what it's like in a red-hot firebox – no Health & Safety in those days.'

Mr Barker adds: 'A regular job for an Aspinall 4-4-0 was the 4.30 am from Central

Station – the "fruit" – consisting of a rake of vans full of produce from Marton Moss, non-stop to Manchester Victoria.'

He even drove Aspinall tanks and 'Dreadnoughts'. 'I've driven them many a time during the night when the foreman had his head down. We used to take them from the coal hole down to the points at Bloomfield Road, then back on the shed.'

Mr Barker, whose home is now in Ingol, Preston, lived in the old station master's house at Layton (then still called Bispham) after his parents moved there in 1926.

'Unfortunately, my Dad died suddenly at the Railway Convalescent Home at Dawlish – his last signal box was Poulton No 3, which I often see now from the road when we visit Poulton.'

* * *

Another veteran railman was Oswald 'Ossie' Aiken, whose 50-year career dated back to pre-Grouping days. He started work as a goods clerk at Ansdell in 1911. The former Kirkham Mayor, who died in 1995 aged 98, had retired in 1961 as goods agent at Blackburn responsible for 10 stations and 250 staff.

With his bowler hat, moustache and carnation in his lapel, Frank Jones looks every inch the archetypal Victorian stationmaster. In fact, Frank was a thoroughly modern

* * *

Two years later there was the passing of a second stalwart of the Fylde's railway scene, with the death at the age of 81 of former British Transport Commission policeman Ronnie Brooke – a 6ft 1in gentle giant known as Big Ronnie. His Fleetwood beat had included two railway stations and the dock estate rail network.

* * *

One hundred thousand spectators – including the new Queen Elizabeth – packed Wembley Stadium for the Coronation Cup Final on 2 May 1953, Blackpool's finest footballing hour. More than 1,000 of those supporters had arrived there thanks to locoman Gordon Harvey, whose special train had pulled out of Blackpool Central that Saturday morning, one of 21 specials that made the journey from Lancashire to London on the historic day.

For Gordon, though, it was to be the way to Wembley woe. The young fireman failed to get a ticket and had to spend the entire match outside the stadium listening to the roar of the crowd inside – without a clue that Blackpool

railman, who believed that British Rail was more customer-conscious than it had been since its formation in 1948. Early in 1993, however, the ebullient rail boss hung up his bowler for the final time after a career that had spanned almost all of those 45 years. He had established a reputation as one of the Lancashire network's most colourful and caring characters – whether organising a station tour for disabled children or helping a Russian runner find his way home from Blackpool. As Regional Railways North West retail manager for Lancashire and Cumbria, Frank was responsible for 347 staff throughout the two counties, including the Fylde Coast.

Born in a railway town – Crewe – he had started his career as a junior porter. One of his key initiatives was to help pioneer CATs – customer action teams – which swing into action to aid passengers if trains break down or are badly delayed.
Lancashire Evening Post

WINTER RAIL SALE
Bargain Off Peak Return Fares Throughout Lancashire and Cumbria
PRESTON - BLACKPOOL WAS £4.20 NOW ONLY £2
BURNLEY - PRESTON WAS £5.30 NOW ONLY £4

Blackpool FC supporters in cloth caps, trilbies and trenchcoats swarm over the platform as a Euston special prepares to leave on Cup Final Day, 2 May 1953. *Evening Gazette*

had beaten Bolton Wanderers 4-3. And the misery was compounded by a nightmarish journey home of no fewer than 8 hours on the footplate of a struggling steam locomotive.

There were, however, two bright spots for Gordon. After the match he unwittingly came face to face with the Queen and the Duke of Edinburgh in their Royal limousine. And the historic result of the Matthews-Mortensen final, in which Blackpool poached victory during injury time after being 3-1 down, soon obliterated any unpleasant memories.

A bitterly disappointed Gordon had seen almost every round of the competition, and as the fireman on one of the specials from Blackpool, he had been confident of picking up a ticket from the Seasiders' fans. But it was not to be.

His day had begun at 3 am when he hauled himself out of bed before cycling from St Annes to the old Blackpool Central shed. The journey to London on a 'Black Five' footplate was relatively smooth, but hopes of securing a ticket soon evaporated when Gordon, whose young wife Eileen was back home in the Fylde, saw the touts were demanding up to 20 times the face value of tickets.

With a handful of other ticketless railwaymen, he stood outside listening to the tantalising cheers and groans from inside. As the crowd surged out after the final whistle, they realised that Blackpool had won. But the joy was to be short-lived: poor-quality coal

meant that the train arrived back in Blackpool 4 hours late. Gordon had been awake almost 30 hours.

He has now recorded his memories of that unforgettable day on tape at his St Annes home – to the accompaniment of authentic sounds of the railway.

Other memories include playing for the 1953 Loco Football Team in the local Wednesday League – competing against police and fire brigade sides – and working with his brother-in-law Peter Hardcastle at Rigby Road MPD in the mid-1950s.

* * *

Pensioner adventurer John Hobson, a former model railway shop owner, journeyed through five continents and 35 countries by train. The Bispham-based septuagenarian's travels included a day trip to Turkey, a 4,000-mile trek across the Soviet Union on the Trans-Siberian Express, and an eventful journey through southern Africa in the days of apartheid. Mr Hobson published a book about his travels.

Since his visits, of course, there have been momentous transformations in both the former USSR and South Africa. There have also been fundamental changes to Britain's railways. But, in whatever form they are owned and operated, the success of the railways still hinges on the dedication of the men – and women – who run them.

MEN AND MACHINES

8.
QUEENS, CLUBS
AND CAMPERS

Rail-borne Royals

The Queen of Coasts has attracted a multiplicity of monarchs over the past 150 years. From the young Queen Victoria's first footsteps in Fleetwood on 20 September 1847, the Fylde Coast has had eight visits by reigning monarchs (though two were *en passant*) and several by kings-to-be. And in almost all of them, the railway played an important role.

When Victoria landed in Fleetwood en route to London from the Western Isles, Sir Peter Hesketh Fleetwood was there to greet her. The Royal Party also included Prince Albert, the Prince of Wales and the Princess Royal. The Queen, who had made Sir Peter a baronet in her first honours list in 1838, presented him with her white kid gloves and a quill pen. An estimated 50,000 people saw the arrival of the

Royal Yacht and its accompanying squadron before the monarch was transported through the Fylde countryside by a Preston & Wyre Railway locomotive on the first stage of the journey back to the capital.

The Fylde had to wait another 66 years for its next visit by a reigning monarch. This time it was George V and Queen Mary on 8 July 1913 in a tour that took them to Kirkham, Lytham St Annes and Blackpool. After being driven along the coast, the Royal couple reached Talbot Road Station, where their train was waiting in one of the arrival platforms.

In 1921 and 1927 there were visits by the Prince of Wales, who in 1936 would become – for 11 months – Edward VIII. But the next visit by a reigning monarch was George VI's tour in 1938. As with his father's visit 25 years earlier, it came on the eve of war, but it did not prevent

A year before the King and Queen's 1913 tour, Princess Louise had visited Blackpool to open the Princess Parade and new sea defences on 2 May 1912. The Princess, who was accompanied by the Duke of Argyle, is seen leaving a decorated Talbot Road Station in the Royal coach escorted by a troop of Horse Guards and with crowds a dozen deep behind the barriers. The handsome ironwork of the station awning can be seen in the background.

Port panorama: the scene in Fleetwood as Queen Victoria and her consort, Prince Albert, prepare to depart from the dock with the Royal children in September 1847. The royal party had arrived from the Western Isles en route back to Buckingham Palace. Crowds of ladies in crinolines and shawls and gentlemen in frock coats and top hats lined the embankment alongside the Royal Train, which travelled along the Preston & Wyre line to connect with the main route to London. It was accompanied as far as Farington by the eminent engineer Sir John Hawkshaw. To the left is Queens Terrace, which still survives. The makeshift nature of some of the trackwork testifies to the fact that it was laid hurriedly beyond the original terminus for the visit, which took place at short notice. The work is dedicated to the port's founder, Sir Peter Hesketh Fleetwood. This engraving by the artist John Eastham is from a daguerreotype taken on the spot.

townsfolk staging lavish celebrations. The King and Queen Elizabeth arrived by train in Colne on 17 May before travelling by car through east Lancashire to Preston and then on to St Annes, Blackpool and Fleetwood, where they left by rail. The port's railway terminus at Queens Terrace was bright with bunting, flags and decorations of heraldic shields. Alongside the platform stood the Royal Train, resplendent in its original cream and maroon livery.

There then occurred an incident that today would have caused a major security flap. As the King and Queen boarded the train, the crowd, anxious for a final glimpse of the couple, surged forward past the police barrier. Hundreds of well-wishers ran to the Queens Terrace railings flanking the platform siding as the train pulled out, and those at the front had a close-up view of the Royal carriage.

George VI and Queen Elizabeth also made two incognito stops in the area during the war. On 28 August 1940 and 30 October 1941, the Royal Train was stabled overnight at Garstang Town Station. As the Royal couple slept, they were protected by police and Civil Defence personnel.

The final official visit by King George and Queen Elizabeth was in 1951, a year before the monarch's death. But it was their daughter's trip to Blackpool four years later that was one of the most momentous Royal visits to the Fylde. The Queen and the Duke of Edinburgh attended a glittering Royal Variety Performance at Blackpool's Opera House. BR took no chances for the visit on 13 April 1955; the Queen and Prince Philip spent the night in the Royal Train in the sidings at Poulton, part of the original P&W line to Fleetwood. A team of workmen relaid and levelled the track so the train would have the smoothest possible ride. Almost 250,000 people thronged the route to catch a glimpse of the 28-year-old Queen and the Duke. Late-night rail services were re-arranged so that the crowds could get home from the celebrations.

Almost 40 years later, however, the Queen broke with precedent for her Blackpool Festival '94 visit: she arrived by plane.

Above Double-headed Class '5' 4-6-0s Nos 45020 and 45045 haul the Royal carriages from the sidings at Poulton during the final official visit by George VI and the Queen in 1951, a year before the monarch's death. *Evening Gazette*

B.R. 14300/79

BRITISH TRANSPORT COMMISSION

C. J. VIDAL
District Operating Superintendent

Telephone
PRESTON 4821
Ex73

Telegraphic Address
DISTROP RAILWAY PRESTON

BRITISH RAILWAYS

DISTRICT OPERATING
SUPERINTENDENT
LONDON MIDLAND REGION
PRESTON

Our Reference
81

Your Reference

Permit Number ___28___

TO ALL CONCERNED.

The bearer, Fireman A. Tomlinson of the

___Motive Power___ Department has

permission to be in the precincts of

Poulton Goods Yard (i.e., the area bounded

by the Public Level Crossing Gates and

Poulton No. 1 Signal Box, including the

Permanent Way Yard) on the 13th and 14th

April, 1955.

THIS PERMIT IS NOT TRANSFERABLE.

CJVidal.

Left and right The locomotives on the Royal Train between Poulton and Darwen on 14 April 1955, after the Queen's visit to Blackpool, were in the charge of two resort-based crews, drivers Walter Somers and A. Smith, and firemen Albert Tomlinson and A. Jackson. Their reward was a letter of thanks and a voucher for 10 shillings (50p) – Mr Tomlinson's is reproduced here by courtesy of his fireman friend Gordon Harvey. They were also given passes allowing them to enter Poulton goods yard, where the Royal Train was stabled overnight.

BRITISH TRANSPORT COMMISSION

S. G. HEARN
Chief Operating Superintendent

S. H. GOULD
Asst. Operating Superintendent

Telephone
EUSTON 1234 Ext.8687.

Telegrams
OPERATING EUSRAIL
LONDON, TASN.

Your Reference

Our Reference SA/W4.

CHIEF OPERATING SUPERINTENDENT
LONDON MIDLAND REGION
EUSTON HOUSE
LONDON, N.W.I

15th April, 1955.

Dear Sir,

I have pleasure in enclosing
a voucher for 10/- (Ten Shillings) to mark
the occasion of your having worked the Royal
Train from Poulton to Darwen on Thursday,
14th April, 1955.

Yours faithfully,

S. G. Hearn

Mr. A.Tomlinson,
Fireman,
BLACKPOOL.

_____

Club trains

The Victorians created the concept of 'Club Class' travel long before it was reinvented by late-20th-century airline operators. For the best part of 50 years, luxurious 'Club trains' conveyed businessmen from their homes in the Fylde to their offices in Manchester and industrial east Lancashire. The daily journey was the opposite of that taken annually by many of their employees – from the inland towns of Lancashire and the West Riding to the ozone-laden air of the Fylde Coast. Merchants and mill-owners could live in salubrious St Annes and commute daily to their workplaces in Manchester and Salford. They did this on board the Club trains – palatial saloon carriages attached to the rear of scheduled services.

The trains were the brainchild of Harold Bowman of St Annes, who in 1895 conceived the idea of what was effectively a mobile gentlemen's club. The proposal was accepted by J. H. Stafford, General Manager of the L&Y, and the Club trains began running on 1 January 1896. Membership of the Blackpool-Manchester 'Club' was by invitation and was restricted to 50 1st Class ticket holders, who jealously guarded their privileges.

The best-known Club trains, linking Blackpool Central and Manchester Victoria, left at 7.18 am and 8.20 am, returning at 5.10 pm and 5.55 pm. In LMS days the 52-mile journey from Manchester to Blackpool could be completed in 1 hr 16 mins. There was also a non-stop Club service for cotton mill managers from Lytham to Rose Grove, serving the east Lancashire textile belt.

In 1991 Regional Railways North West revived the club train concept, although on a more modest scale, with loco-hauled services between Blackpool and Liverpool/ Manchester during the morning and evening rush hours. However, loco-hauled trains were finally withdrawn in 1995, and replaced by diesel units, severing the last link with this long-gone era of luxury train travel in Blackpool.

But not completely: the Manchester

A rebuilt Horwich 'Dreadnought' 4-6-0 travelling at speed hauls a Manchester Victoria-Blackpool Club express in about 1928. The train is on the down fast line on the quadruple track section near Spen Lane, east of Kirkham. *Commercial postcard*

Piccadilly Club train enjoyed a temporary renaissance soon after because of a shortage of 'Sprinter' and Class 158 stock. Class 37s were enlisted to fill the breach into 1996, and also to head the 1995 summer Saturday Blackpool North to Holyhead service. And there was a further loco-hauled link when the late Roy Castle's 'Tour of Hope' train – complete with LMS-style Club saloon, rebuilt by Statesman Rail at Carnforth – paid a whistle-stop visit to the resort in July 1995.

The Blackpool & Fylde Rail Users' Association featured this lament to loco-hauled services, after the withdrawal of the coast's Club trains, in its *Branch Line* bulletin from summer 1995:

'Having faithfully served my passengers for many years,
To think I'm now redundant really drives me to tears.
New-generation multiple units are now the state of the art,
They think I'm too old, too slow, and haven't got the heart.
But I can still beat these upstarts – I'll give them a head start;
No longer will my engine vibrate, my two-tone horn sound irate.
Dumped in a weed-strewn siding, having to await
The cutter's torch, will be my inevitable fate.'

Class 31/4 No 31455 *Our Eli* in platform 5 at Blackpool North, driven by Bill Haddock, after helping to double-head the final loco-hauled train from Manchester Victoria on 26 May 1995. A special headboard marked the occasion. The last Club to Liverpool was hauled the following day by *Our Eli* and No 31439 *North Yorkshire Moors Railway*, with another special headboard. *Malcolm Richardson*

A Class 31 diesel snakes through a spinney of semaphore signals as it heads the final Club train from Liverpool into Blackpool North on 27 May 1995. *Malcolm Richardson*

QUEENS, CLUBS AND CAMPERS

The Caravans, Knott End-on-Sea.

Costa Knott End: less well-known than the Squires Gate campers were these LMS caravan coaches at the terminus of the Garstang & Knott End Railway. This picture is from the 1930s, by which time, ironically, they could not be reached directly by rail.

After the withdrawal of the Knott End passenger service in 1930, would-be campers had to take the train to Fleetwood, then the ferry across the Wyre estuary. *John Ryan collection*

RAILWAYS OF BLACKPOOL AND THE FYLDE

Camping coaches

Camping coaches allowed the railway companies to make use of surplus or obsolescent stock, and families to enjoy a seaside or country holiday in reasonably priced accommodation. Inevitably, Blackpool led the field, with the country's most extensive stock of camping coaches. By 1955 it was the base for no fewer than 15 static carriages, stabled in the sidings at Squires Gate Station. It had the added advantage of being near Blackpool FC's training ground, where young visitors could watch the likes of Stanley Matthews, Stan Mortensen and Jackie Mudie being put through their paces. Squires Gate's closest rival was Abergele in North Wales, with eight campers.

In 1965 the BR Board said that there would be fewer sites that year, many of them having been located on branch lines closed under Dr Beeching's review. His 'Reshaping' report made no specific mention of camping coaches, but from 1969 the LMR was the only Region offering them to the public. By 1971, their final season, the number at Squires Gate was down to a dozen. And then, as more Britons took package holidays abroad and the railways went into retrenchment, there was none…

A unique connection with the golden epoch of the railway was uncovered in the early 1990s in the unlikely location of Borrowash Cricket Club near Derby. A former Blackpool carriage, thought to have been scrapped, had in fact been transformed from Club coach into club pavilion! Built by the L&Y at its Newton Heath Works in Manchester in 1912, Club Car No 47 was ahead of its time, with a modular design, galvanised steel panels and fireproofing modifications. It was withdrawn almost 40 years later, but post-war shortages of building materials ensured its survival as a sports pavilion. In 1993 a group of enthusiasts bought the carriage for a nominal £1 from Redrow Homes, which owns the Borrowash site. The enthusiasts, all members of the L&Y Trust, intended to restore the carriage for special use on the Keighley & Worth Valley Railway. The coach body is believed to be the only surviving example of purpose-built rolling-stock from the Blackpool Club train. *K. Roberts*

9.
BLACKPOOL AT WAR

The Fylde Coast played a central part in Britain's war effort in the two great conflicts of the 20th century. The coast's role was both military – training vast numbers of servicemen and building RAF bombers – and civil – allowing war-weary Britons to relax, recuperate and occasionally revel. And in all this, the railway was the motive force. Blackpool's unrivalled rail links and its distance from the big metropolitan centres made it a relatively safe sanctuary for those seeking a brief escape from the Home Front's front line.

When the First World War broke out, the railway companies were at the peak of their powers. In 1913 the prosperity of the textile industry combined with a superb summer to make it the most successful season so far. The following season promised to be even better, and even the declaration of war on 4 August initially failed to dampen that expectation. The previous day, despite the cancellation of nine Bank Holiday trains because of the European crisis, rail traffic had broken all records. The conflict had been rumoured for so long that its outbreak seemed to arouse less interest than the news that the state had taken over the railways.

During the first week of the war, the L&Y advised holidaymakers to leave Blackpool early as there might not be enough rolling-stock to meet the weekend rush. But no one took much notice of the warning, causing scenes of unprecedented chaos as families scrambled for places on the few trains that ran on the Saturday.

As initial hopes that the war would be 'over by Christmas' began to fade, thousands of visitors cancelled their holidays and the railway

companies cut down their excursions to Blackpool. Landladies were therefore relieved when the Government announced that 14,000 troops were to be billeted in Blackpool for six months. The first troops to arrive were greeted by cheering crowds as they marched out of Talbot Road Station.

As well as the soldiers stationed in Blackpool, the town was also used as a convalescent centre for thousands of wounded servicemen. In October 1915 the King's Lancashire Convalescent Hospital was opened at Squires Gate.

At Central Station, the L&Y brought in its well-equipped ambulance train for the public to inspect. The 'hospital on rails', constructed at the company's Horwich Works, included an operating theatre, wards, pharmacy and mess room. The Red Cross sold dolls in nurses' uniforms for 3s 6d and 5s each towards the war effort. Some of the ambulance train carriages, rebuilt in 1921 by Clayton Wagons Ltd, ended their days on more peaceable duties as seaside camping coaches.

The signing of the Armistice triggered a huge catharsis of pent-up emotion, and Blackpool was one of the main beneficiaries of the desire to put the horrors of war as far into the past as possible.

* * *

As with the Great War, there was a mood of almost unbelievable buoyancy in Blackpool at the start of the Second World War. The 1939 season had seen the completion of a string of major developments, including the Odeon

It was halfway through the First World War, but business continued as usual for Blackpool's bustling railway termini. The concourse at Central Station is a sea of bobbing bonnets and boaters as crowds await their departures in this photograph taken on 19 August 1916. Note the fine display of enamel advertising signs. *Blackpool Central Library*

Cinema, the new Opera House, Talbot Road bus station and Harrowside Solarium. The number of visitors had fallen by 10 per cent in 1938, but 1939 was a boom season as trippers enjoyed a last hurrah before the looming conflict. The number of rail passengers at Easter and Whitsuntide was a fifth up on the previous record in 1937.

Within hours of Prime Minister Neville Chamberlain's sombre speech to the nation on 3 September, however, the railways were being put to an entirely different use. With its huge stock of hotels and boarding houses, wide open spaces on the promenade and sands, vast public buildings and excellent rail links, Blackpool was an inevitable place to billet troops and evacuees from air raid-threatened cities like Manchester. The Government estimated that the resort could absorb an extra 109,000 permanent residents – virtually doubling its size.

Forty-five seafront hotels were commandeered to house civil servants who had been dispersed from Blitz-threatened London; within four months of the outbreak of war, more than 1,700 civil servants had moved to Blackpool. The biggest contingents were from the Ministries of Pensions and National Insurance, but there were several other Departments of State that moved to what had effectively become Whitehall-on-Sea.

On the industrial front, 10,000 Fylde workers were employed at the giant Vickers Armstrong factory at Squires Gate, where they made Wellingtons and other RAF bombers. The first Blackpool-built aircraft flew in July 1940 – assembled in a hangar at the airport while the factory was still taking shape alongside. By the end of the war, more than 3,400 had rolled out. As well as the railway siding near Squires Gate Station, there were also unfulfilled plans in 1941 to extend the tram line a mile down Squires Gate Lane to Common Edge Road to serve the plant.

Mass conscription meant that, for the first time, women were given a chance to work at the sharp end of the railway system. Eleven women left warehouses, factory benches and cafe kitchens in Blackpool to work as goods porters, loading and unloading merchandise in all weathers as it entered and left railway freight yards in the North West. The women, most of whom were aged between 20 and 40 but including a grandmother, worked a 48-hour week, handling everything from tea chests to salt cartons each weighing three-quarters of a hundredweight.

'It's a man's job,' said a railway official, 'but women are doing it, and doing it fine, too.'

The coast was also a vital military complex. RAF Station Blackpool was opened officially in October 1939, and almost 770,000 RAF recruits did their basic training in the resort, joined by tens of thousands of other airmen stationed at RAF Kirkham and RAF Weeton. RAF Blackpool was reputed to be the biggest military training centre in the world, with up to 45,000 airmen housed in 5,000 properties across the town. After Dunkirk this rose to 70,000, and the ranks of the British airmen were swollen by comrades from Poland, France, Scandinavia and Holland. In addition, there were some 10,000 USAAF men based at the huge airfield at Warton (now the British Aerospace plant). US airmen from the big American base at Burtonwood would think nothing of hopping on to a train at Warrington Bank Quay for a night's R and R in Blackpool. The terminals became seething, cosmopolitan melting-pots as different accents and uniforms mingled unselfconsciously in the concourses.

Again, as in the previous conflict, an ambulance train was brought into Blackpool Central; rail enthusiast and photographer Tim Shuttleworth remembers seeing it stored in the carriage sidings when he spent a week in the resort in 1943.

At the outbreak of hostilities, the Government was gripped by a moral dilemma over the ethics of encouraging people to take holidays in wartime. But Churchill and his Cabinet were soon convinced that vacations were a vital morale-booster for a beleaguered population. During the Phoney War the resort was exhorted to continue with its high-profile advertising campaigns. The first Easter weekend of the war was surprisingly busy, but the Whitsuntide Bank Holiday was cancelled after the evacuation of Dunkirk. With every scrap of rolling-stock being channelled into the war effort, there were no special trains at Whitsun nor the next three Bank Holidays.

But the message had failed to get home to a population that was intent on snatching some relief from the dire news of Hitler's blitzkrieg against the Low Countries. On August Bank Holiday 1940, using ordinary, scheduled trains, so many people crammed into Blackpool that some were unable to find accommodation and had to sleep on the sands or streets. The resort enjoyed a significant advantage over most of its main rivals on the East Coast and Channel coast, which had been effectively declared off-limits to visitors because of the threat of invasion or bombardment. In recognition of this, the allocation of locos stationed at Blackpool North and Central sheds, which had been cut to 30, was restored to its pre-war level of 52.

The Fylde and its railways escaped relatively lightly from the war. At 11 pm on 12 September 1940, eight people were killed and 14 injured in Seed Street when a lone Luftwaffe bomber missed its North Station target and released nine bombs. The following year, on the afternoon of 27 August, 12 people were killed outright and six died later in hospital after two British aircraft crashed in the air above Central Station. A Boulton Paul Defiant clipped the rear of a Blackburn Botha, part of which plunged on to the station. The dead included civilians and airmen alike, and 35 people were injured; only moments before the crash, a packed train had left the station. An RAF inquiry attached no blame to the pilot of either aircraft. The names of the civilian victims, and those killed in the bombings in the Fylde, are commemorated on the Roll of Honour of Civilian Dead at Westminster Abbey.

However, the railway system was ready to respond when the end of the war came. Even before VJ-Day, in July 1945 packed trains rolled into Blackpool as the Wakes holidays

Safety by the sea: a classic home front scene as evacuees – and their dolls – arrive in Blackpool by train in the first days of the war. People were still coming to terms with the enormity of Chamberlain's wireless broadcast when the first evacuees began to arrive at Central Station. The bewildered children were greeted by nurses and volunteers at the station barriers. The *Gazette*'s Clifford Greenwood reported on the first's day's arrivals: 'When night fell, Blackpool had been converted in less than 12 hours into a great sleeping nursery'. In the first three days alone, some 37,500 arrived. Within a year, all but 2,200 had returned home, but the exodus to the Fylde Coast began again during the Blitz on Manchester and Liverpool in late 1940. At one stage, more than half the households in Blackpool were being used as billets for evacuees or servicemen. *Evening Gazette*

resumed. The *Evening Gazette* reported: 'Scenes outside Central Station were reminiscent of crowds outside Wembley on a Cup Final day'. A posse of police was on duty at the station gates to control the crowds. Normal service had been resumed.

10.
RAILWAYS TO NOWHERE

The early frenzy of railway mania inevitably produced many projects – ranging from the futuristic to the foolhardy – that never got off the ground. Some of the most ambitious expansion schemes involved bypassing the bottleneck of Preston Station, which handled up to 500 trains a day. Almost all traffic heading to north or west Lancashire had to go via Preston, which gave its joint owners, the L&Y and LNWR, the whip hand in deciding the shape of the county's railway system.

Extensions to the Fylde's tramways were seen as one of the best ways to dodge Preston's dominance. The Blackpool tramway connected with the Lytham St Annes network at Squires Gate and Starr Gate, running from there roughly parallel with the railway. The northern terminus of the blue and ivory Lytham St Annes cars was initially at South Shore Station in Lytham Road.

Though the Fylde is barely 10 miles as the seagull flies from Southport, the wide Ribble estuary meant a 35-mile round trip for anyone wanting to make the journey. A series of schemes was devised for traversing the estuary, including a swing bridge and – most imaginative of all – a 1927 'railplane' crossing plan, using George Bennie's ingenious but costly propeller-driven monorail.

But the scheme that came closest to fulfilment was an innovative proposal in the early 1900s to extend the tramway across the Ribble, partly via a transporter bridge. This would have given a network stretching from the Wyre estuary to Southport, and it could even have been linked from there to the Liverpool system, including the city's overhead railway. A Volks-type 'daddy longlegs' platform, running on rails on the riverbed, would have linked to the transporter bridge across the river channel. There were also later plans for a crossing further upstream towards Preston. However, the practicalities of the plan – and the opposition of the Port of Preston – meant that it never became a reality, though some of the approach tracks were laid.

Another project that got a little further than the drawing office was a scheme to extend the Blackpool tramway from Gynn Square through Singleton to Garstang & Catterall, providing a gateway to the West Coast Main Line. The link was promoted by the backers of the Blackpool & Fleetwood Tramroad Company, who envisaged that the Blackpool & Garstang Railway would gain much of its revenue from goods traffic, especially market produce for Blackpool's millions of summer visitors. It would also have put the unassuming market town of Garstang on no fewer than three lines. The railway would have been run in a similar way to the clifftop tramline between the resort and Fleetwood – as a fast, inter-urban light railway – and if it had gone ahead it could have had a dramatic effect on the development of Blackpool's eastern suburbs. The scheme reached the final stage before construction and the route was even staked out across the Fylde fields all the way to Garstang. But the public would not support the venture – it was by now the early 20th century, and the initial rail euphoria had evaporated – and the line was never built.

The Blackpool & Fleetwood also toyed with the idea of taking over the ailing Garstang & Knott End Railway – and electrifying it – as well as collaborating with the L&Y on a new route into Blackpool, probably with a link at Bispham (now Layton) Station. Both proposals came to nothing.

But there were also expansion plans for conventional rail systems. As early as 1846 the grandly titled Fleetwood, Preston & West Riding Junction Railway sought powers to build a line from the Preston & Wyre to west Yorkshire. It would have run from the Preston & Wyre at Maudlands and linked up with the Preston & Longridge Railway, a 6½-mile branch from the Longridge Fell quarries to Deepdale (whose distinctive stone was used in the construction of Fleetwood docks and the Fylde's sea defences, among other schemes). The line would have stimulated both trade

through the embryonic port of Fleetwood and tourism to the Wyre town, Blackpool and Lytham.

The Preston & Longridge Railway company had been incorporated in 1836 under the chairmanship of Sir Peter Hesketh Fleetwood, the Preston MP and enlightened landowner who also pioneered the line from the town to his Wyre port. The new line would run from the P&W's Maudlands terminus, bypassing Preston Station to the north, and meet the Longridge branch near Deepdale Street. The branch would be widened as far as Grimsargh, from where a new line would run through Clitheroe to Elsack on the Leeds & Bradford Railway to facilitate trade 'between the West Riding and the Colonies, via Fleetwood'.

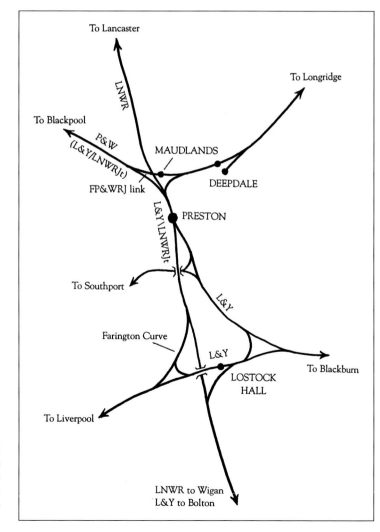

A sketch map showing the FP&WRJ link north of Preston station, and the complex series of junctions and curves south of the station enabling north-to-west trains to pass through Preston (twice!) without the need to reverse.

After a struggle the line was incorporated on 27 July 1846, but it was decided that it should not go beyond Clitheroe, leaving the Blackburn, Clitheroe & North Western Junction Railway to complete the line to the West Riding. It never did. Apart from an isolated excavation near Hurst Green, the only section completed was the 1½ miles of double track connecting Maudlands and Deepdale. Opened on 14 January 1850, this left the P&W near Pedder Street, crossed the main Lancaster line on the level – under the supervision of a crossing-keeper – and soon after plunged into a half-mile tunnel to emerge near St Paul's Road.

The FP&WRJ had leased the Preston & Longridge, only to default on its rent of £3,000 a year, and the Longridge company regained possession in 1852. In 1856, however, the FP&WRJ obtained powers to purchase the Longridge line by instalments for £48,000 from 1 September 1856, under an Act dated 23 June. It was itself absorbed by the LNWR and L&Y jointly on 1 July 1866.

One scheme that did materialise, helping ease the logjam of Fylde services at Preston Station, was the completion of a series of curves and junctions in the Lostock Hall area in 1908. This smoothed the passage of trains from the north, including Scotland, to the Fylde Coast, by avoiding reversing movements in the station. Puzzled passengers waiting at Preston could watch a train pass southward through the station without stopping. Between 15 and 20 minutes – and more than 5 miles – later, it would return heading northward on the opposite side, bound for Blackpool. This was achieved by trains negotiating this complex series of junctions to the south, including Lostock Hall Station and Farington Curve.

A daring £2 million scheme to redevelop Blackpool Central Station was to have started in November 1940. The station would have been replaced by a bigger building in Chapel Street, leaving the land to the north to be redeveloped with car parks, a municipal complex and entertainment centres. War, however, put paid to the plan.

CONCLUSION:
WHITHER THE RAILWAY?

Whither Blackpool's railways? More than a century and a half after trains first ran into the resort, what does the future hold for rail in the town it helped to build? In the brave new Blackpool of motorways and car parks, do the railways even have a future?

As rail in the resort enters the new Millennium, it remains at a crossroads – or, perhaps more accurately, a junction. In the three years since the first edition of this book was published, Britain's railways have experienced enormous and fundamental change. This transformation had been signalled by the former Conservative Government's privatisation experiment, but opinion remains divided about whether the changes are beneficial, and the direction in which they should continue.

In 1993 Parliament approved the Railways Act, which – with the 'Grouping' of 1923 and nationalisation 25 years later – was one of the three major re-organisations of Britain's railway structure in the 20th century. Where there had been a single, necessarily imperfect, nationalised corporation – British Railways – there were now more than 100 companies all interlocked in a complex grid of contracts and franchises. At the heart of the 'new railway' was the Act's most radical proposal: the division of the network between operation and infrastructure. The former was in the hands of the 25 train operating companies (TOCs), the latter in those of the private monopoly Railtrack, which was to charge the TOCs for using its lines. And holding the ring for all these disparate businesses were the Government-appointed Rail Regulator and Franchising Director.

The Fylde Coast is served by four principal privatised operators: North Western Trains (which in late 1998 became First North Western) operating local and regional services; Richard Branson's Virgin Trains (both its West Coast and CrossCountry operations); and Northern Spirit – the former Regional Railways North East – operating the trans-Pennine route. The fluctuating fortunes of NWT have typified the uncertainty about which critics of privatisation had warned. The franchise was initially won by NWT's parent company Great Western Holdings – regarded as one of the more benign and railway-focused TOCs – with promises of 70 new 100 mph diesel multiple units by the year 2000. The first private scheduled train for almost 50 years ran into Blackpool North on 2 March 1997. Barely a year later, however, the company was bought out by bus operator FirstGroup, with some of the departing directors receiving the six-figure pay-offs that had rapidly become the norm in the industry.

Supporters of privatisation heralded the reforms as a reversion to the great swash-buckling, buccaneering days of the early railway pioneers such as Sir Peter Hesketh Fleetwood. More sceptical commentators pointed out that the railway pioneers had taken risks; for a monopoly provider of track and signals, the risk element is hardly the dominant factor.

There have been some benefits from privatisation, including what amounts to a revolution in rail freight, but the lifeblood of the Fylde's lines is passenger traffic. In Blackpool, six years after the town's through service to London was withdrawn by BR, the

Layton Station resembles a bucolic halt in the heart of built-up Blackpool. In February 1994 Regional Railways announced that it was to de-staff the suburban station after 127 years of continuous manning. This followed the decision to make Blackpool North an 'open' station, with tickets checked on the trains rather than at the barriers.

Passenger Martin Wilson gathered more than 160 names on a protest petition, claiming that closure of Layton's ticket office would encourage fare evasion and vandalism, and paying tribute to the lone railwayman who had lovingly staffed the station. BR later announced that it was deferring the de-manning for several weeks for further consultation, but the axe finally fell on 30 May – Spring Bank Holiday – with Regional Railways maintaining that revenue was not covering staff costs.

The station is seen here before and after its platforms were raised to ease access for disabled people. Beyond Crossley's Bridge, which straddles the now-lifted line to the former goods yard, a dilapidated loading gauge stands defiant, silent evidence of how it used to be. *Evening Gazette*

resort acquired no fewer than two direct trains to the capital in May 1998. Richard Branson heralded Virgin's arrival in the resort with typical flamboyance: a mock-up of a mini-Blackpool, complete with miniature Tower and a line-up of showbusiness stars, was on show at Euston Station and the 'first' red-liveried Virgin train ran into Blackpool North on Spring Bank Holiday Monday, 25 May (although the summer timetable had actually begun the previous day). The lavish welcome included a red carpet for passengers, a naming ceremony for the locomotive as *Blackpool Rock*, a jazz band and costume characters from Blackpool Pleasure Beach.

By contrast, North Western Trains opted for a lower-key launch of its daily service between the coast and the capital on the same day. Blackpool's two MPs, Gordon Marsden and Joan Humble, who had been campaigning for restoration of the London link since their election a year earlier, both welcomed the new services.

While Virgin used High Speed Train sets, NWT employed the sleek and comfortable, but limited-capacity, Class 158 'Express' DMUs. Initial loadings on the Virgin version were encouraging, but patronage of its NWT counterpart proved disappointingly low, and there were reports of its future being under threat. Absurdly, the NWT London trains were not allowed to call at major stopping points such as Preston or Crewe because of the 'moderation of competition' rules.

Last of the line. On 28 September 1992, InterCity ended more than a century of railway history when its last direct train to London pulled out of Blackpool North, specially headboarded for the occasion. InterCity blamed poor loadings and plummeting profits. Despite the *Evening Gazette*'s presentation of an 11,000-name 'InterCity Saver' protest petition to BR Chairman Sir Bob Reid in London, with the help of Wyre MP Keith Mans – stressing the importance of a direct rail link to Europe's foremost fun coast – the decision was not reversed. *Paul Nettleton*

However, five years later Blackpool was given a sneak preview of its new Virgin through service to London on an overcast summer's day in 1997. One of the company's freshly painted HST sets visited North Station with a party of underprivileged children on the 'Teddy Bear Special' from London. Class 43 power car No 43092 arrives with the train in platform 1. *Paul Nettleton*

CONCLUSION: WHITHER THE RAILWAY?

Both Virgin and NWT were experiencing significant problems, however. These reached their peak during the Labour Party Conference in Blackpool in September 1998. Ironically, it had been on the first day of the 1992 Labour Conference that the last BR through train to London had run. Since acquiring the West Coast franchise, Virgin had been the target of relentless criticism for late running and general poor performance, which it blamed largely on the rolling-stock and infrastructure it had inherited from BR. A succession of ministers used the conference as a platform to attack Virgin over long delays in services taking MPs, delegates and journalists to Blackpool. Some of the frenzy of anti-Virgin invective was exaggerated and unfair, but it did highlight the consistent under-performance of the company on the flagship West Coast route.

However, the Deputy Prime Minister, John Prescott, persuaded delegates to reject a call from the Rail, Maritime & Transport Union (RMT) for the network to be taken back into public ownership. Instead, he promised a much more rigorous regulatory regime, with consistently poor-performing operators losing their franchises. In other words, privatisation was here to stay, albeit in a more tightly regulated form.

In his Blackpool speech, he also confirmed the pledge in the Government's much-heralded White Paper on integrated transport to form a Strategic Rail Authority to oversee and co-ordinate the system. The Queen's Speech the following month, however, contained no formal proposals for an SRA; instead, a 'shadow' authority would be set up pending legislation to form a fully fledged version.

NWT, meanwhile, was proving to be one of those under-performers that ministers had in their sights, with plans for job cuts and talk of service reductions. Train-crew shortages and rolling-stock reliability problems from the start of the 1998 summer timetable combined to create levels of punctuality and cancellations that were condemned both by the Deputy Prime Minister and the North West Rail Users' Consultative Committee (RUCC). With virtually no slack in the company's fleet to allow for train-strengthening, some of the overcrowded two-car units running between Preston and Blackpool North in the peak holiday season resembled cattle-trucks. The company's new management pledged that it would get to grips with the problems, but there remained a long way to go. Complaints about services in the North West in 1997-98 – the first full year of privatisation – rose by 68 per cent after a declining trend over previous years, many of them focusing on the performance of Virgin, although 1999 saw improvements.

Paradoxically, the much-vilified Railtrack emerged in a more heroic light than the train operators when, in early 1997, it carried out a £2 million re-laying of the South Fylde line between Blackpool South and Kirkham using continuous welded rail on pioneering steel sleepers. The new technology made for a much smoother journey on board the notoriously rough-riding Class 142 'Pacer' units. Railtrack also continued the station modernisation programme in the Fylde that had been begun by BR, including a £700,000 facelift for Blackpool North and the demolition of the dilapidated road-level buildings at Squires Gate Station. Unfortunately, this modernisation has been accompanied by a reduction in staffing hours at some stations, including Kirkham and Poulton. This has led to vandalism, and prompted calls by Malcolm Richardson, Vice-Chairman of the Blackpool & Fylde Rail Users' Association (BFRUA), for staffing hours to be extended as a deterrent.

Preston Station was also being given a refit costing more than £3 million, including refurbishment of platforms 1 and 2 serving the Fylde. But it was the rail infrastructure through Preston and beyond that was creating the most serious problems for longer-distance services to the Fylde Coast. Virgin's plans to run 140 mph tilting trains over the West Coast Main Line (WCML) meant that the 30-year-old infrastructure had to be improved first. To achieve the £2.2 billion upgrade, Railtrack and Virgin agreed an innovative revenue-sharing deal designed to restore the WCML to its former pre-eminence as the backbone of rail services in Britain.

Another longed-for infrastructure scheme was the electrification of the line between

Blackpool, Preston and Manchester, first proposed as long ago as the 1930s. BFRUA and the regional RUCC were consistent and long-term champions of the scheme, but despite successive feasibility studies and proposals it appeared to be little nearer than it had under public ownership.

By the end of 1998 the pattern of services in the Fylde had crystallised. On the Blackpool North line, as well as the two London trains a day – and a new daily through working by Virgin to Edinburgh – the core service remained the hourly train to Manchester Airport, interspersed with a similar service to Buxton via Manchester. Other services included a 2-hourly train to Liverpool, the hourly trans-Pennine to Leeds and York/Scarborough, and Virgin CrossCountry's daily departure to Birmingham and Portsmouth Harbour. In the summer there was also a Saturdays-only train from Holyhead for Irish ferry passengers as well as the successful Dalesrail Sunday service between Blackpool North and the spectacular Settle-Carlisle line via Hellifield. (The Vice-Chairman of the flourishing Friends of the Settle-Carlisle Line, Glynn Hague, lives in Blackpool and has vigorously promoted Dalesrail with a series of illustrated talks about the line – one of which took him to Cambridge University.)

The South Fylde branch continued to enjoy a stability that would have seemed inconceivable in the dark days of the early 1980s, when its future appeared under threat. With an hourly service to Blackburn, Burnley and Colne in east Lancashire, its value was underlined during the 1996 Open Golf Championships when a packed shuttle ran between Preston and the Royal Lytham & St Annes golf course next to Ansdell & Fairhaven Station. Add to this the specials that continued to operate occasionally to Blackpool North, particularly during the Illuminations, and it remained a varied and sometimes even vibrant scene on the two lines.

Privatisation – thanks largely to the dedication of the staff running the railway – has not been the disaster that some Cassandras forecast. But nor has it proved the panacea predicted by many of its supporters. The critical question, however, is not whether privatisation has improved services, but

For air travellers, the new station at Manchester Airport has been one of the biggest boons – and Blackpool has benefited in both directions. Passengers have used the hourly airport service to reach the terminal, and incoming travellers to reach the attractions of the Fylde. Two months before it was opened by the Princess Royal in May 1993, a dozen mayors, including Blackpool's Councillor Dorothy Preston, who sadly died soon afterwards, boarded a Class 150 'Sprinter' for a special preview trip. Rail-air manager Barry Cole welcomes guests to the futuristic station.

On the return journey, pensioner Mel Gaunt inadvertently made a piece of railway history. Mr Gaunt had been on Poulton Station waiting for a train to Blackpool when the airport express pulled in and he was invited to get on board – making him the service's first fare-paying passenger. Soon after his appointment as Regional Railways' area manager for Lancashire and Cumbria in 1995, Mr Cole, a former Blackpool North boss, pledged improved services, spruced-up stations and even better customer care from his 414-strong staff. *Evening Gazette*

whether the improvements could have taken place under the former state-owned system anyway. The train operators receive large, though diminishing, public subsidies. Critics of private ownership contend that if British Rail had been given the same amounts of money as its privatised successors, it could have improved services just as much as, if not more than, the private sector.

Powerful support for this view came from the former Chairman of the British Railways Board, John Welsby, who in 1998 said pointedly: 'If, as a public corporation, BR had been granted the scale of Government funding which is now committed ... we would have thought that the Millennium had not only arrived early but had also brought with it the sort of glorious benefaction that is the stuff of dreams.'

Apart from Virgin's HSTs, rolling-stock is largely Class 158 'Express' units for the trans-Pennine and CrossCountry services, Class 150 and 156 'Sprinters' and 'Super Sprinters' for the Manchester routes, and Class 142 'Pacers' for the South Fylde branch.

In the autumn of 1998, however, there was the return to Blackpool North of a form of motive power that had not been seen there for 30 years. On the rainy afternoon of 17 October, former LMS 'Black Five' 4-6-0 No 45110, preserved on the Severn Valley Railway, coasted into platform 1 with a Pathfinder Tours excursion from Shrewsbury. The jubilant former Secretary of Blackpool Civic Trust, Mrs Ethel Sanderson – whose engine-driver father had once been in charge of the 'Royal Scot' – led a spontaneous round of applause as the gleaming steam locomotive returned to an area with which 'Black Fives' had once been synonymous. And there was a final piquancy that almost seemed to mock the more workaday modern traction alongside the engine: more than 60 years after it was built, the veteran locomotive rolled into the terminus 4 minutes early.

After a gap of 30 years, steam power came back to Blackpool on 17 October 1998 when immaculate 'Black Five' 4-6-0 No 45110 glided into North Station with a Pathfinder Tours railtour carrying more than 400 excursionists. Former Blackpool footplateman Don Rutter greeted the crew in the cab of the locomotive, which, after a circuitous run-round via Preston, hauled the train back to Shrewsbury in the evening. *Barry Shaw*

　　　RAILWAYS OF BLACKPOOL AND THE FYLDE

Above One hundred and one years after its construction in 1894, Blackpool Tower was given railway recognition of its national status by having a locomotive named after it. The then Transport Secretary, Dr Brian Mawhinney, unveiled the nameplate on Transrail Class 37/4 No 37407 at Euston in February 1995, in a ceremony attended by representatives of former Tower-owners First Leisure Corporation. Almost a year later, the loco is pictured in platform 1 at Blackpool North soon after its arrival with a Manchester Club train. *Paul Nettleton*

Below Blackpool Tower made an unexpected return to the resort in March 1997 – on the South Fylde line, which had not seen locomotive haulage for some time. The engine was in charge of a ballast train in connection with the £2 million re-laying of the track on the branch, carried out by Railtrack contractor Fastline. Twelve miles of track were closed completely for a month while contractors used sophisticated road-rail vehicles to replace the old permanent way with pioneering new steel sleepers and continuously welded rail. The locomotive, in the former Transrail livery, has just passed through Squires Gate Station heading towards the Pleasure Beach alongside Raleigh Avenue. *Malcolm Richardson*

CONCLUSION: WHITHER THE RAILWAY?

'Tram on test': the headboard said it all as an £800,000 lightweight tram went on display at an open day at Blackpool Transport Services' Rigby Road depot in July 1998 to mark the centenary of the opening of the Blackpool & Fleetwood Tramroad. The 22-ton 'Roadliner' prototype, seen in the Hopton Road tramshed, was on trial on the Promenade tramway after being transported from Cardiff. The two-car stainless steel vehicle, designed and built by the UK TRAM consortium – an all-British partnership including Blackpool Transport and Blackpool Design Associates – was 29 metres long with wide doors, low floors and the capacity for 200 passengers. In December 1998 a reminder of an earlier tramway era was uncovered – literally – when water-main work in Church Street revealed a short section of the former Marton route, closed in 1962, still in situ beneath the tarmac. *Malcolm Richardson*

BIBLIOGRAPHY

Abell, P. H., Garnham J. A. and McLoughlin, I., *The Tramways of Lytham St Annes* (Oakwood Press, 1995)

Allen, D., 'Seaside Semaphores' (published in *RAIL* magazine, December 1995)

Ashcroft, B., 'Beside the Seaside, 1959' (*Steam World*, July 1990)

Atkins, P., '*Blackpool* – Britain's Most Obscure Locomotive?' (*BackTrack*, January 1996)

Awdry, C., *Encyclopaedia of British Railway Companies* (Patrick Stephens Ltd, 1990)

Biddle, G., *The Railways Around Preston: An Historical Review* (Foxline, 1989)

Blakemore, M., *The Lancashire and Yorkshire Railway* (Ian Allan, 1984)

Brown, K., *Lytham and St Annes: The Reluctant Resorts* (Lancashire County Books, 1992)

Butt, R. V. J., *The Directory of Railway Stations* (Patrick Stephens Ltd, 1995)

Casserley, H. C., *Observer's British Steam Locomotives* (Bloomsbury, 1974)

Clarke, A., *Windmill Land* (George Kelsall, Limited edition reprint, 1986)

Cole, B. and Durack, R., *Happy as a Sandboy: Early Railway Posters* (National Railway Museum, 1990)

Croft, D. J., *A Survey of Seaside Miniature Railways* (Oakwood Press, 1992)

Crombleholme, R. (ed), *Steam '75: the Official ARPS Year Book and Steam Guide* (Haraton, 1975)

Derry, R., 'The Week the Fires Went Out' (*Steam Classic*, August 1993)

Edwards, M., *The Garstang-Knott End Railway* (Lancaster Museum monograph, 1980)

Eyre, K., *Seven Golden Miles* (Dalesman, 1989)

Gammell, C., 'Walking to Shap' (*Steam World*, January 1994)

Grime, A. (ed), 'A Scientific Survey of Blackpool and District' (prepared for the Blackpool meeting of the British Association for the Advancement of Science, 1936)

Harris, N. and Ashcroft, B., 'Dignity and Defiance' (*Steam Railway* supplement, May 1993)

Hentschel, O., 'Preston Station Survey' (*British Railways Illustrated Annual No 3*, Irwell Press, 1994)

Hesketh, P., *Trams in the North West* (Ian Allan, 1995)

Holt, G. O., *A Regional History of the Railways of Great Britain, Vol 10: The North West* (David & Charles, 1978)

Hooper, R. (ed), *The Fylde Story* (Glasgow & Associates for Fylde Borough Council, 1988)

Hudson, J., *Wakes Week* (Alan Sutton, 1992)

Jordan, A. and E., *Away for the Day* (Silver Link Publishing, 1991)

Kirkman, R. and van Zeller, P., *Rails to the Lancashire Coast* (Dalesman, 1991)

Marshall, J., *The Lancashire and Yorkshire Railway*, Vols 1, 2 and 3 (David & Charles, 1969, 1970, 1972)

McCartan, S., *Revoe for Ever* (published by the author, 1995)

McLoughlin, B., *Railways of the Fylde* (Carnegie, 1992)

McRae, A., 'Camping Coaches on Britain's Railways' (*BackTrack*, July-August 1994)

Mitchell, W. R., *By Gum, Life Were Sparse! Memories of Northern Mill Towns* (Warner, 1993)

Nock, O. S., *British Locomotives of the 20th Century*, Vol 1 (Patrick Stephens Ltd, 1983)
    The Lancashire and Yorkshire Railway: A Concise History (Ian Allan, 1969)

Orchard, A., *Blackpool North Pier Tramway* (Lancastrian Transport Publications, 1992)

Palmer, G. S., *North Station and Fleetwood 1897-1963* (Blackpool & Fylde Tramway Historical Society, 1963, reproduced by S. Palmer and Lancastrian Transport Publications, 1993)

Palmer, S. and Turner, B., *Blackpool by Tram* (Palmer & Turner, 1968)

Palmer, S., *A Nostalgic Look at Blackpool Trams, 1950-1966* (Silver Link Publishing, 1995)

Poole, R., *The Lancashire Wakes Holidays* (Lancashire County Books, 1994)

Porter, J., *History of the Fylde of Lancashire* (W. Porter & Sons, 1876)

Potter, T., *Reflections on Blackpool* (Sigma Leisure, 1994)

Ramsbottom, M., *A Journey from Preston to Fleetwood in the 1850s* (Hedgehog Historical Publications, 1991)
    The Preston and Wyre Railway (Hedgehog Historical Publications, 1991)

Rothwell, C., *Blackpool in Old Photographs* (Alan Sutton, 1994)
    Lytham St Anne's in Old Photographs (Alan Sutton, 1993)
    The Preston and Wyre Railway (Winckley, 1991)

Rowledge, J. W. P., 'Aspinall and Hughes Express Passenger Locomotives of the Lancashire and Yorkshire Railway' (*Locomotives Illustrated*, March-April 1993)

Rush, R. W. and Price, M. R. C., *The Garstang and Knott End Railway* (Oakwood Press, 1985)

Rutter, D., 'The Glorious Years' (*Steam Railway*, November 1993)

Shannon, P. and Hillmer, J., *British Railways Past and Present: No 3, The North West* (Silver Link Publishing, 1986)

Turner, B. and Palmer S., *The Blackpool Story* (Palmer & Turner, 1976)

Walton, J. K., *The Blackpool Landlady: A Social History* (Manchester University Press, 1978)
    Wonderlands by the Waves (Lancashire County Books, 1992)

Welbourn, N., *Lost Lines: LMR* (Ian Allan, 1994)

Wilson, M., *Tramlives No 1 – Stan 'The Tram' Croasdale* (Lancastrian Transport Publications, 1994)

Wood, A. W., and Lightbown, T., *Blackpool in Old Picture Postcards* (European Library, 1983)

Wray T., 'Blackpool Central Station Survey' (*British Railways Illustrated Summer Special No 1*, Irwell Press, 1993)

Files of the *Evening Gazette*, Blackpool, the *Blackpool Gazette and Herald*, the *Lytham St Annes Express* and the *Blackpool Times*.

INDEX